Let's declare a holiday!
A holiday for the whole world.
Death is defeated.
Access to God is opened.
Man's greatest enemy is conquered;
man's greatest opportunity is made possible.
Of course we should celebrate!
And celebrate we do, not just once a year
but every week. On Sunday.
That's when God's people gather
to celebrate the Resurrection.
Yes, we "gather" to celebrate.
Whoever heard of solitary celebration?
How can we really enjoy good news by ourselves?
The people who know the risen Christ
want to get together
to remember and to rejoice.

CHURCH-
WHO
NEEDS
IT?

DAVID ALLAN HUBBARD

A Division of G/L Publications
Glendale, California, U.S.A.

Scripture quotations in this book are from the Revised Standard Version, copyrighted
1946 and 1952 by the Division of Christian Education of the NCCC in the U.S.A.,
and used by permission.

© Copyright 1974 by G/L Publications
All rights reserved.
Printed in U.S.A.

Published by
Regal Books Division, G/L Publications
Glendale, California 91209, U.S.A.

Library of Congress Catalog Card No. 73-90622
ISBN 0-8307-0285-7

CONTENTS

Gift-Marie Wholey 1989

PREFACE

We could learn a great deal about a person's priorities from his or her prayers. Most of the time, however, prayer goes on in private, the secret conversation between the worshiper and God.

Happily, we are not left to guess at the contents of the greatest prayers in history. They have been preserved for us in the New Testament—the prayers of Jesus Christ. From His prayers, we learn His priorities.

At the beginning of His ministry, with His disciples freshly recruited, he taught his young church to pray. At the close of His ministry, with His disciples now seasoned for service, He prayed for His church. These two prayers—recorded in Matthew 6 and John 17—disclose His priorities, priorities which center in worship.

The word *church* is troublesome, because it has several meanings, most of which appear in these chapters. Sometimes *church* is used to describe the whole company of men and women on every continent, in every century, in heaven and earth, who have trusted God through Jesus Christ and so become God's people, forgiven of their sins, reborn by God's Spirit, blessed with eternal life.

At other times *church* means the local building in a given community where persons who profess or aspire to be Christians gather to worship God and learn about their faith.

Most of the time *church,* in this book, means a local congregation, the assembly of people who convene to express their worship, to enjoy their fellowship, to prepare for their mission and to enlarge their understanding. In city, town, neighborhood, or countryside, they are the particular expression of that larger universal church which will one day be assembled before God's throne.

It is the role and purpose of this regular gathering with the local congregation which is the burden of these talks. The final chapter was given—in somewhat different form—as a commencement address at Pasadena College, Pasadena, California and at Malone College, Canton, Ohio. It was also one of the presentations at Explo '72 in Dallas, Texas. The other talks were first heard on "The Joyful Sound" broadcast.

When all is said and done, our Lord's priorities will become ours. To claim His Lordship and spurn His priorities is an impossible contradiction. To examine these priorities and the prominence they give to worship with the local congregation is the task of this book. Its *timeliness* is made clear by the amount of present discussion about the church and the reasons which many—even Christians—give for non-participation. Its *timelessness* is assured by the subject matter: the prayers of the eternal Lord are never out of season.

WHAT IS WORSHIP?

The next day he saw Jesus coming toward him, and said, "Behold, the Lamb of God, who takes away the sin of the world! This is he of whom I said, 'After me comes a man who ranks before me, for he was before me.' I myself did not know him; but for this I came baptizing with water, that he might be revealed to Israel."

And John bore witness, "I saw the Spirit descend as a dove from heaven, and it remained on him. I myself did not know him; but he who sent me to baptize with water said to me, 'He on whom you see the Spirit descend and remain, this is he who baptizes with the Holy Spirit.' And I have seen and have borne witness that this is the Son of God."

John 1:29-34

1 WHAT IS WORSHIP?

COMMEMORATION OF CHRIST'S DEATH

In every city in America people were dancing in the streets. There were no strangers, let alone enemies, among them. They slapped each other in joy like long lost friends. They embraced each other warmly like members of a family at an annual reunion. Cheers and songs flooded the August night, and millions of hands raised to the sky the "V" for victory sign we had learned from Winston Churchill.

The war was over. The seemingly endless months of conflict from September 1939 to August 1945 were finally at an end. The long nights of waiting, the hard days of wondering were over. Lands overrun with enemies were liberated. The squandering of human life had ceased.

Resources previously dedicated to destruction could now be devoted to peace and health. Hundreds of thousands of families could have their daddies, sons and brothers home again. And those that could not, took satisfaction at least in the knowledge that others would not now have to die. The sorest problem of the century had been solved. And celebration, high celebration, was in order.

The years of cold war and the bitter struggles in Korea and Viet Nam have taken the edge off the sharp memories of that night in August 1945. It has taken its place in history along with November 11, 1918, when our parents celebrated the close of a war that was to make the world safe for democracy.

Great days these were, cosmic in their scope, monumental in their significance. The fact that we no longer remember them with full enthusiasm shows that there are other problems yet to be solved. At the time they happened Armistice Day and V-J Day loomed colossal like Mount Everest. Now they have merged with many other mountains in the range of dramatic historical events. We remember them and even celebrate them. But they no longer have the ultimate significance we once attached to them.

In fact the ultimate celebration, the truly high holiday takes place every week. Not in observation of a military victory but in commemoration of a man's death. On every continent, in virtually every country, from the barren icy wastes above the Arctic Circle to the coral islands of the South Pacific, from Filipino barrios to Park Avenue penthouses, men and women gather week by week to remember a Man who died.

It is in church that this grand commemoration takes place. To understand why, we have to go back to a scene early in the public ministry of Jesus. John the Baptist, who was Jesus' second cousin, was six months older than Jesus and began his ministry first. Announcing that God's kingdom was at hand and baptizing men and women who wanted to repent, John had gathered a number of followers before Jesus had any disciples.

One day Jesus came to the spot by the River Jordan where John was baptizing. John "saw Jesus coming toward him, and said, 'Behold, the Lamb of God, who takes away the sin of the world!' " (John 1:29). The staggering truth of that statement draws millions of people to church every week.

The Fulfillment of God's Program

Underlying John's stunning declaration about Jesus is his firm belief that in Jesus all of God's program was heading for fulfillment. It would have been easy for John's followers to make a mistake right here. They could well have thought that Jesus was another itinerant teacher giving his own interpretation of God's law from town to town. They might even have felt threatened, as though he were a competitor to John and his ministry. All this John forestalled when he paid tribute to Jesus.

"The Lamb of God," John called Jesus and pointed to the Old Testament preparation for the Christ. The minds of John's hearers undoubtedly went back to that night of destiny in Israel's history when a lamb made all the difference. Judgment was slated for the land of Egypt where the Israelites were living as slaves. To escape the judgment each Israelite household was to slay a lamb and sprinkle its blood on the door frame outside their house.

"For I will pass through the land of Egypt that night, and I will smite all the first-born in the land of Egypt, both man and beast; and on all the gods of Egypt I will execute judgments: I am the Lord. The blood shall be a sign for you, upon the houses where you are; and when I see the blood, I will pass over you, and no plague shall fall upon you to destroy you, when I smite the land of Egypt" (Exod. 12:12,13).

The blood of a lamb saved each family from death. When John called Jesus the "Lamb of God," some who heard would have remembered the sacrifices described in Leviticus: "If he brings a lamb as his offering for a sin offering, he shall bring a female without blemish, and lay his hand upon the head of the sin offering. . . . and the priest shall make atonement for him for the sin which he has committed, and he shall be forgiven" (Lev. 4:32,33,35).

6

The sacrifice of a lamb meant forgiveness to the sinner.

John's friends would also have recalled Isaiah's description of God's suffering servant when Jesus was identified as the Lamb of God. "He was oppressed, and he was afflicted, yet he opened not his mouth; like a lamb that is led to the slaughter, and like a sheep that before its shearers is dumb, so he opened not his mouth. . . . Yet it was the will of the Lord to bruise him; he has put him to grief; when he makes himself an offering for sin, he shall see his offspring, he shall prolong his days; the will of the Lord shall prosper in his hand; . . . by his knowledge shall the righteous one, my servant, make many to be accounted righteous; and he shall bear their iniquities" (Isa. 53:7,10,11).

The death of a righteous man who is likened to a lamb works the will of God and brings righteousness to many.

These three pictures from Exodus, Leviticus, and Isaiah form the background for John's stupendous statement. It is as though the Baptist gathered up all the strands that speak of sacrifice for sin and wove them together. He proclaims Jesus as God's true Lamb, the great sacrifice to which the sacrifices of the Old Testament pointed.

When we go to church we commemorate the fact that Jesus died to fulfill the plan for our salvation—a plan that God laid out even before He created the world. As we gather week by week we salute Jesus Christ as the One who fully carried out God's program to call a people out of sin into fellowship with Him. Whether we gather to sing the old gospel song,

"Look to the Lamb of God," or to hear a mighty chorus lift the strains of, "Worthy Is the Lamb That Was Slain," we are acknowledging together that in Jesus all that God intended for our salvation was accomplished.

And that's why we go to church.

The Solution to Our Greatest Problem

"Behold, the Lamb of God, who takes away the sin of the world" (John 1:29). Not only does John the Baptist find in Jesus the One who fulfills God's program, he sees Him also as the One who solves our greatest problem, the problem of sin.

The depths of God's solution is seen in the verb John uses—"takes away." Contrast this with the verbs that we so often use to deal with sin. We *hide* sin, burying it carefully in the undergrowth of our lives, camouflaging its grave against all discovery. Or we *deny* sin, when it is discovered, making excuses, blaming other persons protecting ourselves by pleading ignorance.

When we see sin in those we love, we often try to *escape* it, by running away from the problem. We parents, particularly, have difficulty in acknowledging it when our children are in trouble. For most of us, sin is so puzzling that our response to it is confused at best. Sometimes we rationalize it; sometimes we resist it; sometimes we revel in it. But it is always there, the nagging, negative fact of our existence.

When we think how sin dogs our actions, clings to our thoughts, spoils our motives, John's word is comforting. Jesus is the Lamb of God that "takes away the sin of the world." In our worship Sunday by Sunday we rejoice in the depths of God's solution to our problem of sin.

And we remember the scope of God's solution as well. Jesus, God's sacrifice, takes away the sin "of the world." Our minds boggle at the thought. Our own sins are so overwhelming that we can't comprehend how anyone could cope with the sin of the world. But the infinite, eternal Son of God did. The whole world may not be saved, but it will not be because Christ's sacrifice is not sufficient or because His power is limited.

Because Christ died for our sins, our sins can no longer destroy us. Because Christ died for our sins, forgiveness is possible, a way to God is opened, fellowship with God can be enjoyed.

And that's why we go to church.

With God's people we join regularly to worship God by commemorating our Saviour's death. As we do, we also appropriate fresh grace. The sacrifice that Christ made never loses its power. Whatever we have said or done or thought does not take us beyond the reach of that grace. The love that led Christ to lay down His life as the Lamb of God will not let go of us.

Remembering Christ's death and appropriating fresh grace remind us that we can expect complete deliverance from all that sin has done to us. Other victories we have known have been partial and incomplete. We celebrate the end of one war and wait nervously for the beginning of another.

But the victory that God's Lamb achieved in taking away the sin of the world is complete. We see its full results in the book of the Revelation. "And between the throne and the four living creatures and among the elders, I saw a Lamb standing, as though it had been slain . . . and . . . the four living creatures and the twenty-four elders fell down before the Lamb . . . and they sang a new song, saying, 'Worthy art thou to take the scroll and to open its seals, for thou wast slain and by thy blood didst ransom men for God from every tribe and tongue and people and nation, and hast made them a kingdom and priests to our God, and they shall reign on earth'" (Rev. 5:6,8-10).

Why go to church?

To commemorate the death that made this kind of victory possible. And to enjoy something of the peace and fellowship of that final victory ahead of time. Christ solved our gravest problem and calls us to enjoy His solution to the full.

And that's why we go to church.

Gracious Father, teach us just how grateful we ought to be. The very sin Christ came to save us from sometimes keeps us from seeing how great that salvation really is. Give us strength to gather with Your people to remember, to learn, and to await the whole meaning of Your love. Through Christ who loves us and gave Himself for us, we pray. Amen.

The Passover of the Jews was at hand, and Jesus went up to Jerusalem. In the temple he found those who were selling oxen and sheep and pigeons, and the money-changers at their business. And making a whip of cords, he drove them all, with the sheep and oxen, out of the temple; and he poured out the coins of the money-changers and overturned their tables. . . .

The Jews then said to him, "What sign have you to show us for doing this?"

Jesus answered them, "Destroy this temple, and in three days I will raise it up."

The Jews then said, "It has taken forty-six years to build this temple, and will you raise it up in three days?"
John 2:13-15,18-21

2 WHAT IS WORSHIP?

CELEBRATION OF CHRIST'S RESURRECTION

All the world loves a holiday. A change of pace, a respite in the routine of life, a chance to celebrate a memorable event—for all these reasons, and more, men and women everywhere look forward to holidays.

It would be hard to go any place or find any people without holidays. For some, holidays are tied to the seasons, like the great midsummer festivities in Scandinavia or the midwinter carnivals in Minnesota. For others, holidays remember great historical events, especially days of independence or liberation from tyranny, like Bastille Day in France, Cinco de Mayo in Mexico, or the Fourth of July in the United States.

Though all the world loves holidays, there is no holiday that is really worldwide. Most holidays are anchored in national or tribal traditions or tied to the history of a specific group. In a sense, holidays are in-group celebrations. They have deep significance for those who observe them but very little meaning to anyone else.

What would it take to get the nations of our globe to establish a world holiday? Perhaps if inhabitants of Mars or some other point in outer space tried to invade our planet and we banded together and repelled them, we would set a world holiday. But that's a pretty remote possibility because we have no good reason to believe that there are inhabitants in outer space.

Maybe if some brilliant scientist were to come upon a remedy for pollution we would mark off a day in his honor. A pill to purify our lakes and streams, a spray to purge our atmosphere of smog—these would call for a high holiday and a worldwide one at that. But this too is undoubtedly wishful thinking.

Our problems in ecology will not be solved in one fell swoop by some stroke of chemical genius but by patient application of sound controls and by a surrender of the selfishness that leads to exploitation.

There is no world holiday yet, nor will there be for a long time to come, if man's efforts are to bring it about. Maybe that's the clue: man's efforts are not enough. If our deepest human problems are to be solved, we must look beyond man. And this is the help that the New Testament gives us.

The scene was a strange one, hardly the kind of spectacle that seemed world shaking. It was Passover time in Jerusalem, and Jesus, like all good Jews, headed for the capital city. He found the Temple teeming with activity.

Here is John's description: "In the temple he found those who were selling oxen and sheep and pigeons, and the money-changers at their business" (John 2:14). The sacrifices for Passover required animals, and many of the pilgrims had come too far to bring their own with them. They may even have had foreign coins with them that needed changing before they could buy their animals.

The whole picture deeply offended the Master. "And making a whip of cords, he drove them all, with the sheep and oxen, out of the temple; and he poured out the coins of the money-changers and overturned their tables. And he told those who sold the pigeons, 'Take these things away; you shall not make my Father's house a house of trade' " (John 2:15,16).

Not the stuff of which great holidays are made, is it? But as we see its full significance we may change

15

our minds. Much more was involved than a rash gesture to rid the Temple of its commercial activities. The Jews found this out when they questioned His right to impose His will on the whole Temple community: "What sign have you to show us for doing this?" (John 2:18). Their voices rang with resentment at Jesus' rash intrusion. They demanded to know what miracle He has worked to demonstrate His divine authority.

Jesus' answer was calculated more to confuse than to clarify: "Destroy this temple, and in three days I will raise it up" (John 2:19). The Jews mocked Him in disbelief. They thought He was talking about the magnificent structure built by Zerubbabel and refurbished over a forty-six-year period by King Herod the Great. But Jesus had another temple in mind, and it is this temple that gives this scene its global significance.

A New Way to God Is Opened

The old Temple, built first by Solomon in Israel's heyday and then rebuilt after Nebuchadnezzar leveled it just before the Exile, was the center of Israel's religious life. More than any other place, it symbolized Jewish law. The feasts, the fasts, the sacrifices, the regulations, the priesthood all focused in the Temple.

When Jesus cleansed the Temple He was confronting the whole religious establishment head on. He was opening a new way to God. Not only did He purge the Temple, He made it passé. John makes this plain. When Jesus drove out the peddlers and the money-changers He also drove out the animals.

Let's look at that text again: "He drove them all, with the sheep and oxen, out of the temple" (John 2:15). The sacrificial system was to be abolished. Jesus Himself was to be the new sacrifice, the new way by which men could approach God despite their sin.

Sheep and oxen had served their purpose in God's program. They had enabled Him to pass over the sin of His people, until Christ would come to deal with it permanently. The sheep and oxen were herded out of the Temple by the Lamb of God who had come to do completely what animals could only do in part.

To open this new way to God, Jesus not only drove out the animals, He offered His own body as the new temple, the new sanctuary of true worship. He does this when He shifts the attention of His hearers from the Jerusalem Temple to His own death and resurrection.

The sign of His authority, His right to speak for God, is that His body will be destroyed and raised up in three days. At the time the people missed His meaning, "When therefore he was raised from the dead, his disciples remembered that he had said this; and they believed the scripture and the word which Jesus had spoken" (John 2:22).

For Jesus' friends the Resurrection became exactly what the Jews had asked for—an amazing sign that God was doing something extraordinary through Him. He had a right to change their worship. He was sent from God to do just that. He had the power to displace their Temple. He was acting under the orders of the Lord who built it in the first place.

The evidence of Christ's power and authority was His resurrection.

His resurrection was also the evidence that God had accepted His sacrifice and granted our forgiveness. Paul's brief summary helps us understand this. He says that Jesus was put to death because we had trespassed against God and that Christ was raised because we have been justified (Rom. 4:25).

A new way is opened with a new sacrifice and a new temple. Gone the fear and superstition. Gone the meticulous restrictions and oppressive regulations. Access to God through Jesus and Him alone is possible.

Let's declare a holiday!

"Therefore, brethren, since we have confidence to enter the sanctuary (the presence of God) by the blood of Jesus, by the new and living way which he opened for us through the curtain, that is, through his flesh, and since we have a great priest over the house of God, let us draw near with a true heart in full assurance of faith . . ." (Heb. 10:19-22).

This "full assurance of faith" which the author of Hebrews rejoices in is what we express when we gather to worship in Jesus' name. Jesus Christ's crucifixion and resurrection have dealt a death-blow to our fear of approaching God. God has shown Himself to be for us, and we come to Him in confidence. Jesus has opened the new way.

The Power of Death Has Been Defeated

The scene that began when Christ took whip in hand and went for the money-changers and the animals comes to its climax with the announcement that

18

death has been done in: "Destroy this temple, and in three days I will raise it up." A stupendous claim, the Jews thought, looking at the magnificent stones that graced the lavish structure.

But Jesus' declaration was even more startling. Death itself would be defeated. His own body would struggle with and defeat man's last enemy. The matchless power of God would crush the power of death.

Life itself would be transformed. The long, dark shadow cast over every man would be removed. That final terror which wads up life's plans and throws them in the wastebasket half finished would be erased. That grim reality which snatches loved ones in their prime and leaves us to mourn in bitter emptiness would be swept aside. Resurrection, not death, has life's last word.

Let's declare a holiday!

A holiday for the whole world. Death is defeated. Access to God is opened. Man's greatest enemy is conquered; man's greatest opportunity is made possible.

Of course we should celebrate!

And celebrate we do, not just once a year but every week. We may not have an official world holiday sanctioned by the governments of the globe. But we do have Sunday. It comes as close to a world holiday as anything we have. In almost every land, and in almost every town in every land, God's people gather to celebrate the Resurrection.

"Gather" is the key word here. Whoever heard of solitary celebration? People who celebrate by themselves are usually sick, huddling in some corner bucking up their spirits with alcohol. How can we really enjoy good news by ourselves? The people who know the risen Christ want to get together to remember and to rejoice.

Talk about holidays—Easter combines the warm memories of Memorial Day with the high hopes of the Fourth of July. Sin and death have been soundly beaten. Man's worst enemies have been set aside.

That's why we go to church.

Is church going out of style?

Not as long as we remember that every Sunday is Easter, the day of hope and resurrection. No reluctant moping as we go to church, no halfhearted holding to a habit, but exuberant rejoicing in all that Christ has done.

He is risen; sin is put down; death is defeated. Friendship with God is possible.

Let's start celebrating and then keep at it week after week after week.

Heavenly Father, why is it that we either celebrate things that aren't worth it or we don't celebrate at all? Make us different. Change us. Open our eyes to see the meaning of Jesus' resurrection. As His dead body threw off the grave clothes that bound it, so help us to throw off the fearful attitudes that keep us from rejoicing in the risen Savior. Let His power bring health and wholeness to our broken lives. In His mighty name, we pray. Amen.

When Jesus had spoken these words, he lifted up his eyes to heaven and said, "Father, the hour has come; glorify thy Son that the Son may glorify thee, since thou hast given him power over all flesh, to give eternal life to all whom thou hast given him. And this is eternal life, that they know thee the only true God, and Jesus Christ whom thou hast sent."
John 17:1-3

FELLOWSHIP
WITH THE
ONLY TRUE GOD

People go to church for all sorts of reasons. Many of the reasons are not very sound. For some, it is force of habit; for others, the fear of rejection by church-going friends. Still others go to keep in touch with acquaintances and to enlarge their circle of business contacts.

And if people go to church for all sorts of reasons, they also stay away from church for all sorts of reasons. Almost all of them bad. The preaching is not intellectually stimulating, the music is boring, and the liturgy dull. The congregation is unfriendly, and the pews uncomfortable. The trustees are always talking about money, and the minister's wife does not dress the way I think she should. Besides, Sunday is the best day to watch football and basketball on television.

For some, the reasons for staying away from church are more subtle. They are sincere Christians whom I have in mind. They meet with neighbors every Friday night for prayer and Bible study, and the fellowship is so rich that they get more out of that evening than they do the Sunday service. Young people, particularly, enjoy the periods of discussion that these groups afford. Preaching seems like a one-way street to them. No opportunity to question or comment.

Around the country there are thousands, perhaps scores of thousands, of small groups meeting to share their faith and to grow in their relationships with Christ. Youth groups, college groups, couples, professional people—doctors with doctors, engineers with engineers, teachers with teachers. Wonderful, these groups. One of the most encouraging spiritual signs of our day. But they should not be substitutes for church.

Is church going out of style?

It is not, and it must not. For God's people to assemble regularly in various places is part of God's plan for history. We must not tamper with it. If the New Testament does not push hard for church attendance, it is because it cannot imagine that anyone would try to be a private Christian.

The author of Hebrews was aware of some problems, but his exhortation is the exception, not the rule: "And let us consider how to stir up one another to love and good works, not neglecting to meet together, as is the habit of some, but encouraging one another, and all the more as you see the Day drawing near." (Heb. 10:24,25).

Jesus Himself surely intended that His followers gather regularly for worship. At the beginning of His ministry Jesus gave His disciples a prayer to use in their public worship. Its plural form—our Father, our bread, our debts—is a clear indication that it was intended for groups.

The disciples were to pray when they met together. And at the end of His ministry Jesus prayed for His disciples as a group. From beginning to end it was His church that Christ had in mind.

Jesus' prayer in John 17 gives us an unparalleled look at what is important to Him. As He faces the cross Jesus opens His heart to His Father in prayer. He centers His prayer in the relationship between His disciples and His Father. In other words, worship was a chief concern of His prayer. Not that He speaks about it explicitly but it is woven into everything He says.

As Jesus moves from theme to theme in His prayer, which is the longest recorded prayer we have from Him, He touches on many facets of worship. These themes furnish our topics as we continue our study on the importance of our church attendance.

Why is church going so vital to our Christian lives? It helps to mark us off from the world, while preparing us to minister in the world. It is part of our obedience to God's truth. At the same time church attendance is an expression of Christian unity. Christ begins His prayer in John 17 by describing worship as fellowship with the only true God.

I suppose there are as many foolish statements made about religion as about any other subject. You may have heard some of them.

"All religions say essentially the same thing."

"There are many roads to God."

"It doesn't really matter what you believe as long as you are sincere."

"Each religious faith is just right for those who believe it."

"What you believe is not important. It's how you treat your fellowman."

These themes, with major and minor variations, are played with increasing regularity at dinner parties, luncheon clubs, and campus rap sessions. But people who make these statements have never really heard what Jesus Christ has said. Oh, they may honor Him as a great religious teacher, a superb example of love and integrity. But they have missed His most important words—His claim to be the only bridge between God and man.

An Exclusive Fellowship

We know God only through Jesus. "Father, the hour has come; glorify thy Son that the Son may glorify thee, since thou hast given him power over all flesh, to give eternal life to all whom thou hast given him" (John 17:1,2).

Brash words, these. Jesus is either telling the solemn truth, or we have to brand Him mad. There is no middle ground.

Can you sense how stupendous His claims really are? Staring His hour of death square in the face, He speaks of glory. Badgered by His enemies and misunderstood by His friends, He talks of having authority over all flesh. With His life about to be snuffed out by a grim plot, He boasts the power to bequeath eternal life to others.

Only Jesus has this kind of glory, this amazing authority, this staggering gift of life. And as He mentions life, He pushes His claim one step further: "And this is eternal life, that they know thee the only true God, and Jesus Christ whom thou has sent" (John 17:3).

Truth or blasphemy are our only options here. Without hesitation or embarrassment Jesus links His name to God's as the giver of eternal life.

No wishful thinking about the truth of all religions here. Christian worship is exclusive. We worship in Jesus' name, or it is not the true God we are worshiping. Jesus' point cuts sharp. Any old worship will not do. God has not left us on our own to worship

27

as we will. He has sent His Son with the exclusive right to introduce men to God.

We Christians have met God through Jesus, and that's why we go to church.

An Ultimate Fellowship

Jesus' description of God leads us to an important observation. "The only true God" is the phrase Jesus uses, and as He does He tells us that our fellowship with God is not only exclusive, it is an ultimate fellowship.

Fellowship can be defined simply as the sharing of experience with a person. Since the person with whom we share our experiences in worship is the only true God, this is an ultimate fellowship. There can be no higher, no richer relationship.

What do you want from another person in fellowship? Ability to listen? Understanding? Concern? Support? Encouragement? Acceptance? Wisdom? Counsel? Honest evaluation? Loving correction? Total commitment to your welfare? Take all of these ingredients of friendship and multiply them by infinity, if you want to have some idea of what fellowship with the only true God means.

Knowing God means worshiping Him, acknowledging His uniqueness, confessing our sin and failure, appropriating His grace, thanking Him for His goodness. Of course, we can do this privately. But where we best enter into the meaning of this ultimate fellowship is when we assemble with others who know this true and living God through Jesus Christ.

"Blest be the tie that binds our hearts in Christian

love; the fellowship of kindred minds is like to that
above."

A Fruitful Fellowship

Our fellowship with God, which we express together in worship, is exclusive. Only through Jesus
Christ do we truly know God. And our fellowship
with God is the ultimate in fellowship because the
only true God, the Lord of the universe, thoroughly
loving, totally capable, is the one we have come to
know.

Then, too, our fellowship with God is fruitful. It
leads to eternal life. Twice in this passage Jesus calls
attention to this: ". . . thou hast given him power
over all flesh, to give eternal life to all whom thou
hast given him. And this is eternal life, that they
know thee the only true God . . ." (John 17:2,3).

The fellowship that Jesus makes possible is not just
a passing acquaintance, not just a casual friendship.
It sharply and brightly transforms our lives and our
destinies. It links us to God's own life.

Now we shall miss the point if we think of eternal
life only in terms of its duration. Last it does, forever.
But it does more than last. It catches us up in the
very life of God. The kingdom, power. and glory of
the eternal God we share in right now. The love,
peace, and joy which only God can give are a present
possession, not just a future legacy.

To know God is to live differently, to be changed
radically. One of the reasons that we gather regularly
with other Christians in worship is to give expression
to the new life that we together share.

Is church going out of style?

Not as long as men and women, boys and girls, know the only true God. No other experience so effectively expresses and enriches our fellowship with God as does public worship. This exclusive, ultimate, fruitful fellowship is too important to keep to ourselves. It needs sharing. And our fellowship with Jesus grows and develops through sharing.

Have you ever known a person quite well and afterwards met his family? It is amazing how much we can learn about a person by knowing his family. We see he gestures like his dad, he smiles like his mother. We understand his pattern of speech as we get to know his brothers and sisters. From his family we learn more about the person we thought we knew well.

So it is with God. Meeting with His family, with the people who name His name and know His love, we learn clearer lessons of grace. What He is has rubbed off on them. They will never be the same again. And neither will we as we take seriously our fellowship with them and with Him.

Heavenly Father, what a privilege it is to know You. We have it on good authority that this knowledge means a new kind of life. What Christ's authority has declared, our experience makes clear. Thank You for this life. Thank You, too, that we don't live this life by ourselves. Teach us to enrich our fellowship with members of Your family. In Jesus' good name, we pray. Amen.

"I am praying for them; I am not praying for the world but for those whom thou hast given me, for they are thine; all mine are thine, and thine are mine, and I am glorified in them. . . . I have given them thy word; and the world has hated them because they are not of the world, even as I am not of the world. I do not pray that thou shouldst take them out of the world, but that thou shouldst keep them from the evil one."
John 17:9,10,14,15

4 WHAT IS WORSHIP?

SEPARATION FROM THE WORLD

The human family is divided into two great groups, two distinct entities. Not just male and female, though those are wonderful categories. And not just children and adults, though these age groupings add spice to life. Not just left-handed and right-handed, Republicans and Democrats, rich and poor.

The most basic distinction which human society knows is the difference between the church and the world. To miss this difference is to ignore one of the great realities of life. The distinction between the church and the world is not the result of an arbitrary decision made by Christians. It is not an expression of ingroup pride, of *them* and *us* divisiveness. In fact the church has often tried to rub out this distinction or to draw it incorrectly.

The distinction between the church and the world was first made by neither the church nor the world. The church did not make it out of defensiveness or snobbery. And the world did not make it out of spite or anger.

The distinction between the church and the world was made by Jesus Christ, who read clearly the basic composition of human society. This difference is not just psychological as though based on emotional reactions. It is not just sociological, as though tied to our behavior as groups or families. It is theological in the literal sense of the word: it has to do with our understanding of God.

"And this is eternal life," Jesus prayed, "that they know thee the only true God, and Jesus Christ whom thou has sent" (John 17:3). This exclusive, intimate, ultimate relationship not only links Christians to God, it cuts them off from the world.

Now let's not get this wrong. *World* in this context has little to do with geography. It has everything to do with attitude toward God. The world, as Jesus used the term here, is the vast company of people who do not yet know the true God.

As Jesus prays, His cross looms large before Him: "Father, the hour has come" (John 17:1). He is ready to finish His work and return to the Father with whom He had been from all eternity.

"And now I am no more in the world, but they are in the world, and I am coming to thee" (John 17:11). Christ's chief concern in these last hours is the relationship between His disciples and the world. Time and again, it is this theme that is on His heart as He converses with His Father.

Separation from the world and penetration of the world are the twin centers around which this relationship pivots. Detachment yet involvement, withdrawal yet engagement—this is the rhythm expressed in this prayer. If ever careful listening to Christ were necessary, it is just here. To miss His meaning is to doom ourselves to compromise or irrelevance.

The church's struggle has always been to be enough in touch with the world to speak to its needs without being so much like the world that we have nothing to say. Few passages will help us more in dealing with this dilemma than John 17, our Saviour's own analysis. As usual, our authority will be Jesus Christ. He knows best who the church and the world really are and how they differ.

The Special Providence for the Church

"I have manifested thy name to the men whom

thou gavest me out of the world; thine they were, and thou gavest them to me" (John 17:6). This is how Jesus begins His prayer of concern for His people, His church in the world. What marks the church off from the world is a special providence, a unique provision that God has made for the church.

Given by God—this is the first distinctive of the church. And it is a magnificent one. God has reached down into the family of man and laid hold of some of its members. By His sovereign and merciful hand He has given them to His Son Jesus Christ.

If someone asks you why you are a Christian, try this for an answer: "I'm a Christian because God has given me to Jesus Christ."

Now I know that many of you can remember the time you yielded to the gentle pressure God put upon you. You said "yes" to His call; you raised your hand in a meeting; you knelt by your radio. But remember this, whatever part you had in this decision takes second place to God's, who gave you to Christ and, so doing, separated you from the world.

Committed to God's program—this is the second distinctive of the church, the second way that God's special providence has shown itself.

Let's listen as Christ continues in prayer: "Now they know that everything that thou hast given me is from thee; for I have given them the words which thou gavest me, and they have received them and know in truth that I came from thee; and they have believed that thou didst send me" (John 17:7,8).

This last clause is a key: "they have believed that thou didst send me." Our commitment as Christ's church is expressed in the verb "believed," which might be paraphrased as, "bet our lives," "staked all we are and have." It means we have banked on what God is doing through Jesus.

This venture of faith centers in God's program—He *sent* His Son. The world looks at Jesus in curiosity, even in wonder but fails to acknowledge who He is. The church sees Him as God's Son, sent by the Father to deal with our most desperate problems.

This commitment to God's program is *specific*, not vague. It is based on God's own words, given to us by Jesus. There's a lot of mysticism in the air today, a lot of uncertain religious sentiment. God and Jesus are getting a lot of headlines, and it is the going thing to talk about spiritual experiences. But much of this is far too vague to be recognized as biblical.

God's program, to which the church is committed, is not just a set of inner yearnings, not just an empty religious longing. It has been described specifically in God's own words, given to us in the Bible. It involves God's call of Abraham, His rescue of Israel from Egypt, His kingdom under David, His incarnation in Jesus who died and rose again, His coming in glory to write history's last chapters.

Christ's words outweigh all our spiritual feelings. They decide what we do or do not believe. And they are specific.

This commitment to God's program is *intelligent* as well as specific. More than once Jesus stresses the part that knowledge plays in it. "Now they know that everything that thou hast given me is from thee . . . and they . . . know in truth that I came from thee" (John 17:7,8).

Not "feel," "wish," or "hope" is the verb, but

"know." Our minds are involved. Information is vital. Facts are essential. These the Bible has given the church. Away with hunch and intuition. God has spoken, and His people can know!

This commitment to God's program will prove *successful*. We have Christ's word on it. Of His amazing relationship with God and with the church Jesus says, "All mine are thine, and thine are mine, and I am glorified in them" (John 17:10). A startling statement. The church has scarcely come to birth, and Jesus affirms that He is glorified in His people.

When we remember that Jesus' own glorification had to do with His triumphant accomplishment of the Father's will, we catch the full impact of this promise. The church will not fail. They will make Christ's glory known in the world just as Christ by His obedience made His Father's glory known.

Cared for by Christ—this is the third distinctive of the church that God has marked off from the world by His special providence. Given by God, committed to God's program, cared for by Christ—no room to feel sorry for the church here. The church has a high privilege, a marked destiny.

Note how Jesus prays for His own. "I am praying for them; I am not praying for the world . . ." (John 17:9). Think what it means to have Jesus pray for you. Jesus, at God's right hand, mentions your name in prayer.

The Sharp Reactions from the World

But it is not blessing alone that marks the church off from the world. It is also the world's hostility. "I have given them thy word; and the world has hated them because they are not of the world . . ." (John 17:14).

True Christian faith cuts across the grain of what the world stands for. The church has a new allegiance—the only true God and Jesus Christ whom He sent. This means that whatever the world worships smacks of idolatry.

And the church has a new system of values—love for neighbor becomes the way of life. This means that man's deep-rooted selfishness is exposed. Not that the church obeys the two great commandments to perfection. Only Christ did that.

But the church with its new allegiance and its new values has begun to discover the true meaning of life. And the world finds this discovery unsettling. It wants so much to be right and fears that it may be wrong. And it shows its fear in hostility. It tries to protect its own life-style by putting down the church. But Christ keeps the church, and that's all the defense she needs.

Is church going out of style?

Not on your life. Christ gave Himself to separate us from the world. Not a separation of fear and anxiety, mind you, but a separation of blessing and hope.

One of the reasons that we as God's people gather in hundreds of thousands of congregations throughout the world is to remind ourselves that Christ has made us different. And in this difference lies the meaning of life.

Holy Father, Jesus' prayer prompts us to pray too. If He needed to bring His concerns before You, how much more do we? We cannot add a great deal to His prayer that we recognize our difference from the world. But we can say "amen" to it, because we know that what He prayed for is best for us. So we say "amen" and "thank you" in His name. Amen.

"As thou didst send me into the world, so I have sent them into the world. And for their sake I consecrate myself, that they also may be consecrated in truth."
John 17:18,19

PREPARATION FOR MISSION IN THE WORLD

Christian worship goes on in the midst of the real world. We praise God in our kitchens; and by our bedsides we seek His help in our daily plans. And our churches have street addresses just like those of banks and department stores. Third and Main, Hill and Broadway, 1125 South Central—these addresses remind us that we do not spirit ourselves away to clandestine retreats to worship; we do not don spiritual robes and gather on a quiet mountainside. We walk or drive to the church behind the courthouse or beside the supermarket. The same streets that lead to church take us to school, to office, to factory, to store.

It should be this way. God is with us in the midst of our days. His presence is not confined to religious occasions or sacred shrines. He has left His church in the world, and in the world He welcomes the worship of that church.

Let's hear how Christ puts this in His prayer: "And now I am no more in the world, but they are in the world, and I am coming to thee. Holy Father, keep them in thy name . . ." (John 17:11). And again, "I do not pray that thou shouldst take them out of the world, but that thou shouldst keep them from the evil one. They are not of the world, even as I am not of the world" (John 17:15,16).

The church is *in* the world but not *of* the world. "In the world" in the sense that we live among the human family and together we form a society which spins through space on this whirling planet of ours. But not "of the world" because our allegiance is to the only true God and our value systems have been transformed so that our basic aim is to do His will.

44

Think of the church and the world as two circles. Some would keep these circles completely separate so that they never touch, like two bracelets lying side by side on top of your dresser. This is extreme monasticism. We have no contact with the world in order to preserve ourselves from contamination by the world.

Others would take the two circles and overlap them slightly like round links in a chain. The circles would touch at a couple of points but be largely separate. After all we do have a few things in common with the world—we wash our clothes at the same laundromat and buy our food at the same market.

But there is a better way to picture the relationship between the church and the world than with separated circles or slightly overlapping circles. Christ views the church and the world as concentric circles. A smaller circle inside a larger one, like a bull's-eye in a target.

The smaller circle is inside the larger circle, yet separate from it. Just so the church is in the world, yet separate from it. And one of the reasons we gather to worship God in our local congregations is to demonstrate our separation from the world.

The Pattern of Our Penetration

But that's only part of the story. Christ's prayer in John 17 makes it clear that our relationship to the world is one of penetration as well as separation. Our ultimate goal is not just to preserve ourselves intact by keeping the world from corrupting us; it is to involve ourselves with the people of the world so that their lives are changed by our presence among them.

"As thou didst send me into the world, so I have sent them into the world" (John 17:18). Christ's statement is blunt. He wastes no words. The church is not only being *left* in the world with the will to survive; it is being *sent* into the world with the order to advance. Offense, not defense, is the strategy.

"Sent" is the crucial verb here. It links the church tightly to God's great program in history; it ties us into God's great secret for which the world was made. Notice the way in which the verb sent is used. In verse 3, life eternal comes by knowing God and Jesus whom He has sent. In verse 8 the essence of the church's commitment is captured in the words "and they have believed that thou didst send me." At the heart of history's meaning is the great mission of God—He *sent* His Son.

Now in the same way, Jesus sends His church into the world to make known the Father's loving name. In life and in speech the church becomes part of God's grand scheme to bring men and women back to Him in worship and obedience. That wondrous rescue operation by which God was pleased to conquer our rebellion, to surmount our foolishness, to overcome our idolatry is carried on now by the church.

Within the larger circle of the world, the inner circle, the church, is to push out its circumference, to enlarge its diameter and embrace the peoples of the world with the love of Jesus Christ. The pattern for our penetration is clear. God laid it out when He loved the world and sent His Son.

The Power for Our Penetration

This prayer of Jesus mentions the power for our

penetration into the world as well as the pattern for it. "And for their sake I consecrate myself, that they also may be consecrated in truth" (John 17:19).

We should probably connect this consecration that Jesus mentions with His statement in verse 1 that the hour of His glory has come. It is the cross that is on His mind. For Him the hour of glory is the hour of His supreme obedience to God in giving up His life to make life possible for us.

He consecrates Himself to the cross, as His highest act of love and devotion. He sets Himself apart—that's what consecrate means—to do God's will whatever the cost. And His consecration gives us power for our consecration.

Diversion, distraction is our greatest enemy. That dire combination of apathy and selfishness opens us regularly to seduction. Life is geared to lead us away from God's will, and we are programmed to follow.

What is it that can keep us steady? What is it that can help us turn a deaf ear to the siren songs that seek to lure us aside? It is the power of Christ's cross, with all that His magnificent death conveys.

His consecration means that our failures can be forgiven. Venturing into the world for Jesus Christ is risky business. Mistakes we will make. Failures we can expect. But that high hour when the Son of God was pinned on a bloody stake is our assurance that God will not let sin destroy His program. As members of Christ's church we can launch our excursions into the world with the full confidence that God has already dealt with our mistakes when Christ consecrated Himself for our forgiveness.

His consecration furnishes us with a shining example as we seek to penetrate the world. He was sold out to His Father's will, totally dedicated to His Father's program. And to this kind of dedication He calls us.

Our commitment to follow Jesus into the world and do His will there takes priority over all other allegiances including family ties: "He who loves father or mother more than me is not worthy of me; and he who loves son or daughter more than me is not worthy of me; and he who does not take his cross and follow me is not worthy of me. He who finds his life will lose it, and he who loses his life for my sake will find it" (Matt. 10:37-39).

The daily reminder of Christ's cross gives us the power to take ours and venture into the world for His sake.

The Prospects for our Penetration

Jesus does not close His prayer without a word of encouragement. The inner circle, the church, is not going to shrink, shrivel, or collapse under the pressures from the outer circle of this world. To the contrary. The growth, the expansion of the inner circle is going to make constant inroads on the world. The prospects for penetration are high.

Here are Jesus' hopeful words: "I do not pray for these only, but also for those who believe in me through their word, that they may all be one; even as thou, Father, art in me, and I in thee, that they may also be in us, so that the world may believe that thou has sent me" (John 17:20,21).

Did you catch the way Jesus pictures the expanding circle? "Those who believe in me through their word" is the way He describes the growth of His church. And how it has grown! From eleven on the eve of His crucifixion, to one hundred twenty in the upper room, to three thousand at Pentecost, to thousands more in the book of Acts, to hundreds of millions from virtually every nation on every continent.

The world has been penetrated by the church and still is being penetrated. Almost daily we hear accounts of men and women whose lives have been radically altered by Christ and His gospel. Wealthy people and street people, influential people and obscure people, young people on our sophisticated university campuses and older people in the remote tribes of South America or New Guinea.

Now the situation is ripe for us to move forward even more rapidly in the penetration of the world. There is a spiritual hunger in our land almost without precedence in our history. I find a greater openness to the words of Christ today than ever in my lifetime.

Is church going out of style?

Not a bit. Our patterns of worship may change, our organizational structures may be revised. But the church is as important as ever. It is commissioned by Christ to carry on His mission. As we meet regularly with other members of Christ's church we are preparing for our part in the penetration of the world.

The Word of God that we hear as we gather weekly instructs us in the pattern for our mission. It shows us what God is doing in history and our part in it. The preaching of the cross supplies part of the power for our mission.

We confess our sins and receive forgiveness. We

are reminded of Christ's dedication and renew our own. Fellowship with other Christians encourages us that God is at work forcing back the frontiers of skepticism and claiming new groups of worldlings as His own.

And that's why we go to church.

Father, You have told us not to love the world or the things of the world. Yet You have also told us that You loved the world so much that You gave Your Son for it. Help us as members of Your church to know the deep meaning of both these statements. Free us from love of worldly goods and fascination with worldly attitudes. Yet free us by Your forgiveness to love the people we know in the world that in our love Your love may come through loud and clear. In the name of the church's living Lord, we pray. Amen.

"Sanctify them in the truth; thy word is truth."
John 17:17

OBEDIENCE
TO GOD'S TRUTH

Truth comes high on the open market. And it should. It's worth a lot. In a world where falsehood is a way of life, where it's hard to sort out fact from fiction, where mistakes come naturally, truth is rare enough to command a high price.

In science, for instance, huge amounts of time, energy, and money are expended in the quest for truth. In thousands of laboratories on hundreds of university campuses and other centers for industrial research, the search for truth goes on.

Electronic microscopes peer into the intricacies of life. Cyclotrons blast matter into tiny bits so that we can find out what it is made of. Experiments are repeated scores of times to check their reliability. And all for the sake of truth, which for the scientist means an accurate and verifiable understanding of what the universe is made and how it works.

In the field of history, the situation is a little different. Repetition is impossible. Events happen in the past and are gone. We have no laboratories in which to reconstruct and analyze them. Instead we pour over documents, dig in the ruins of ancient cities, retrace the steps in history between now and then to catch the connections.

When we have verified our facts as fully as possible and worked out close correlations between them and other historical events, we go one step further. We try to find patterns which will help to explain why events took the course they did. In books by the thousands and museums by the hundreds, diligent historians have stored their information. A tribute to the value of truth.

In drama and literature, truth is the sensitive portrayal of how people feel and what they do with their feelings. Novelists and storywriters seek to probe motives, to expose the conflicts that rage within us, to lay bare the emotions that impel us to do what we do. And as we read their books or watch their plays we discover something of ourselves.

The best of these works are a combination of searchlight and mirror. They clarify what's going on around us, while giving us a good look at ourselves. When the book or play touches on motives that we struggle with or insights that we share, we say, "That's true."

When the Bible speaks of truth, it puts a premium on it that goes beyond anything known in science, history, and literature. Jesus' words in His prayer for His church speak for themselves: "Sanctify them in the truth; thy word is truth" (John 17:17).

This view of truth is unique—unique in origin, unique in purpose. Unique in origin because truth is linked to God's Word. Unique in purpose, because truth is given to produce holiness.

Obedience in the Midst of the World

Think again of the church and the world as two concentric circles. The church is the smaller circle inside the larger circle of the world. The difference between the church and the world is clear. The church is comprised of those who know God and Jesus Christ whom He has sent. They have been given by God to Christ and have become part of God's plan to make His name known throughout the world.

The church is that part of the family of man that is set apart to obey God. And this obedience goes on in the midst of the world. That larger outer circle is constantly pushing against the inner circle seeking to perforate it and engulf the church in idolatry and selfishness.

This continual threat means that the church needs constant reinforcement to maintain its distinctiveness. It has to be reminded regularly of who it is, to whom it belongs, and what it is to be doing. In each of these areas the world is working against it.

In the midst of the world the church is threatened by self-doubt because of the world's hostility. Of the church Jesus says, "I have given them thy word; and the world has hated them because they are not of the world, even as I am not of the world" (John 17:14).

It is hard to be hated. No normal group wants others to think badly of it. Insecure as we are, we can easily have our poise shaken, our confidence rattled by the fact that the world opposes our faith and rejects our commitment.

Being part of the church in the world is a little like joining a baseball team that plays all its games in the other team's stadium. The crowd seems always against you. It cheers your mistakes and rejoices in your misfortunes. Your clutch hit or sparkling defensive play is greeted by hostile silence. The partisan fans are pledged to your defeat. No wonder the church needs the encouragement of God's truth to keep its mind on its mission.

In the midst of the world the church was threatened by self-pity because of Christ's departure. All that these first Christians knew about their faith they had learned from Jesus. In all things godly He had been their teacher. But now the world's hostility was mounting; their own ranks were confused and unsure; their leader was leaving. They could feel almost as though they had been seduced and abandoned. It might have been easy for them to drift back into the world and there salve their self-pity.

Even at a distance of nineteen centuries we can feel their problem. The heroes of the world are tangible and visible—politicians, athletes, entertainers, millionaires. Our hero is in heaven unseen, unheard, unsung. How we need God's truth to keep our loneliness from rubbing out the line that separates us from the world!

When Jesus asked His Father to set His church apart from the world by its obedience to God's truth, He knew that the church could be threatened by self-righteousness because of its achievements. Jesus had promised success. The church was going to make an effective invasion of the world. Others were going to believe through the word of the first apostles. And this very success might prove a temptation.

After all it is part of the pattern of the world to take credit for its successes, to feel proud of its achievements. The church had to unlearn this pattern. All credit for achievement must be laid at God's feet. His were the kingdom, the power, and the glory.

Only what is done in His strength and for His name's sake really counts.

Any other approach to success spells failure. Christian pride can punch holes in that inner circle that separates us from the world and let the world's arrogant attitudes flow in and corrupt. That is why we need to hear the truth of God's Word and obey it.

Obedience to the Truth of God's Word

"Sanctify them in the truth; thy word is truth" (John 17:17). We obey God where we are, where He has placed us in the midst of the world with all its temptations. That's our first point.

Our second is this: It is the truth of God's Word that we are called to obey.

Our sanctification, our separateness from the world, is not of our own doing. When the church erects its own barriers, sanctifies its own customs, canonizes its own heroes, all we have is another form of worldliness.

The church has no power to make itself holy. Only the holy God, whom Jesus addresses as "Holy Father" and "righteous Father" (John 17:11,25) can do that. Christ prays for our sanctification, knowing that the Father alone can bring it about.

Error we find on every hand. It is life's most available commodity. That is why truth is so important. We misunderstand the nature of reality and need science to come to our rescue. We misread or neglect our past and must have the historian's help. We deceive ourselves about our inmost motivations until the novelist or playwright holds his mirror before us.

But where we go wrong even more is in our understanding of God. Here we make the great error. Here truth is utterly indispensable. What separates the church from the world is the true knowledge of God in Jesus Christ.

This knowledge, however, is ever under assault. The old idolatrous ways insistently push in on us. The line between church and world is ever in need of repair. Only the truth of God can provide a buffer against this erosion.

The truth of God's Word reminds us steadily of who God is. It shows how inadequate are our own ideas, how deceptive are the symbols that we create to represent Him. It judges our misconceptions and straightens out our confusion. And more than that it guards us from ultimate failure.

Mistakes we make every day. But God's truth, as we obey it, guards us from the grand error—the error of making ourselves or something else God. The church, through her living Saviour, has come to know who God is. And the truth of God's Word keeps us in that knowledge.

One of the great purposes of our public worship is to reaffirm our obedience to God's truth as it comes to us in Scripture. Together we hear the truth as it is read to us. Together we seek to apply the truth as it is preached to us.

Together, I say, because there is strength in numbers. Pressure from the world, doubts about our mission, insecurity because of Christ's departure from the world—all these tend to aggravate our sense of loneliness. If the world can divide us, it may come close to conquering us.

Is church going out of style?

Not a bit. Think what it means to be lost, hopelessly disoriented in a strange city, unable to read the signs or find the way. Then a stranger who speaks your language not only gives you directions but walks along the way with you.

Think what it means to be cut off from news of loved ones who live in a disaster area where hurricane has blasted or earthquake rocked and then to hear that they are safe. Think what it means to be frustrated in working out a problem, income tax instructions for instance, and then have an expert come and show you how.

As long as error is our way of life, church will be in style. It is the society of those who for special purposes are set apart from the world by the power of God's truth. I am pleased, by God's grace, to be counted among them.

And that's why I go to church.

Father, when we hear Christ praying for His church, we are overwhelmed with a sense of its importance. And to think that we are part of that company for whom He prayed and still prays! Let no error in our lives, no idolatry or selfishness hamper the fulfillment of that prayer. Set us apart for Your worship and service by the truth of Your Word. Teach us to quit playing with our obedience and to be as serious about it as Jesus was, when He went to prayer in the shadow of the cross. In His holy name. Amen.

"And now I am no more in the world, but they are in the world, and I am coming to thee. Holy Father, keep them in thy name, which thou hast given me, that they may be one, even as we are one. . . .

"I do not pray for these only, but also for those who are to believe in me through their word, that they may all be one; even as thou, Father, art in me, and I in thee, that they also may be in us, so that the world may believe that thou hast sent me. The glory which thou hast given me I have given to them, that they may be one even as we are one."
John 17:11,20-22

EXPRESSION
OF CHRISTIAN UNITY

There they stand on corner after corner—our churches. Almost every rural wide-spot has two or three, though one may now be closed or converted to an antique shop. And our cities seem to have as many churches as gasoline stations.

Read the church page in our Saturday newspapers and you find almost as much variety as in the automobile advertisements. Nowhere in the world is the church more diverse than in the United States, although Africa with its hundreds of small denominations is a close second.

There are several reasons for this diversity. It is partly historical and geographical, sometimes tracing back well before the Reformation to divisions in the Catholic church. We speak of Eastern and Western branches of Catholicism. The Eastern churches with their centers in Greece, Syria, Russia, Turkey and Eastern Europe, we call Orthodox. The Western branch we know as the Roman Catholic church.

At the Reformation several branches of Protestantism were formed, for both geographical and doctrinal reasons. Lutherans became dominant in Germany and the Scandinavian countries, including Finland. The Reformed churches, which counted John Calvin as their great leader, held sway in Switzerland, the Netherlands, and Scotland.

Closely related to the Reformed churches was the Anglican church which split from Rome at the time of Henry VIII. Out of the Reformation too came the Anabaptist groups, especially the Mennonites who refused to bear arms and held that only true believers should be baptized.

Through the centuries after the Reformation other

groups were formed. Congregationalists and Methodists moved away from their Anglican heritage, while Covenanters and Free church groups separated from the Lutheran church in Sweden.

These divisions were compounded when immigration to America took place. Not only did most of these groups take root in the New World, but they did so at various stages in history. Groups that came later often refused to join their brethren who had migrated a few decades earlier. The newer immigrants felt that the more settled groups had become too Americanized in language and culture, so they held themselves aloof and tried to conserve their old-world ways.

Rugged individualism along with geographical and doctrinal differences helps to account for the variety of denominations on our soil. Strong-willed leaders broke away from parent groups and took their followers with them. The branches of Wesleyanism are numerous, and Baptist groups are legion.

Racial differences, sad to say, have helped to divide the church. Well before the American Revolution there were separate black denominations, and at the time of the Civil War several great denominations split between north and south along a religious Mason-Dixon line.

This welter of church groups forms a strange backdrop for the words of Jesus' final prayer for His followers: "Holy Father, keep them in thy name, which thou has given me, that they may be one, even as we are one" (John 17:11).

One people of God in the midst of the world—this was the theme of Jesus' prayer. Like a smaller circle within a larger circle, the church is in the world—deliberately placed there by Jesus Christ. But that smaller circle is in danger of rolling up into little balls, tiny circles clustered together in the midst of the larger circle of the world.

The Model for the Church's Unity

The real danger the church faces is not that it will meet in different groups. It has to do that. Geography alone dictates that Christians meet with other Christians who live near them.

Almost from the beginning the church was divided by distance. Only at Pentecost could virtually all who were Christians in the whole world be together. And immediately after Pentecost the church was dispersed.

But dispersion is not the main danger facing the church—competition is. The real danger the church faces is that every group will think it is the only group that is right. We must take our convictions seriously without becoming sectarian. Our deepest Christian loyalties must be to Christ and the Scriptures, not to our own sense of rightness.

At least three times in His prayer in John 17 Jesus gives us a model for the church's unity. Let His words sink in. "That they may be one, even as we are one."

And again, "that they may all be one; even as thou, Father, art in me, and I in thee, that they also may be in us."

And once more, "the glory which thou hast given me I have given to them, that they may be one even as we are one." (See John 17:11,21,22.)

The intimate, eternal relationship between the Father and the Son is the model for Christian unity.

The exact meaning of this comparison is hard to come by, because it takes us to the heart of the mystery of God's own nature: the Holy Trinity—one God, three persons. Yet the force is terribly clear. The closest union known in heaven, the oneness of the Father with His Son, is to be mirrored on earth in the oneness of all who serve the Father and the Son.

The least that this means is that *Christian unity is not optional.* We do not have the choice of accepting or rejecting other Christians. Our oneness is a given commandment—based on the fact that we all belong to the same God, if we know the Son whom He has sent.

This model of our unity also means that *it is not merely functional.* We do not seek to work and worship together just for the sake of efficiency. Rather, it is part of the very nature of the church that we belong to each other because we belong to Christ.

For Father and Son to be separated from each other is unthinkable. So also it is unthinkable that Christians should live in isolation when at the heart of Christ's concern is our oneness.

The Extent of the Church's Unity

Christ did not limit His concern to the circle of His first disciples. Of course, He wanted them to get along together. But He went far beyond that. The extent of the church's oneness is shown in His prayer for those who later were to come to know God.

Remember how Jesus put this: "I do not pray for these only, but also for those who believe in me through their word, that they may all be one" (John 17:20,21).

"Those who believe in me through their word."
That's an all-embracing clause. It includes you and
me if we have believed.

That first crew of Christians with their special
commission to spread the word about Jesus, apostles
we call them, were like a pebble dropped in the pond
of the world. Their influence has flowed in ever larger
circles to the farthest shores. All of us have been
reached by someone who was reached by them.

We are some of the latest links in a chain that
stretches back to that first handful whom Christ chose
as His men. We are some of the newest twigs on
an ancient vine whose roots are sunk in the soil of
the biblical events.

All God's people are to be one—those past and
present, those alive on earth and those alive with
God in heaven. Our bright joy and awesome responsibility is to live in terms of this oneness.

The Purpose of the Church's Unity

Our unity is tightly bonded to our mission. Our
oneness has important things to say to the world.

"The glory which thou hast given me I have given
to them, that they may be one even as we are one,
I in them and thou in me, that they may become
perfectly one, so that the world may know that thou
hast sent me and hast loved them even as thou hast
loved me" (John 17:22,23).

Christ's approach is strong and direct, though we
dare not call it simple. What the world needs to know
is God's love. Christ gave clear demonstration of
God's love in His life and death in the world. After
He rose from the dead and returned to His place

by the Father's side, it became the task of the church to make God's love clear among men.

Hardly anything can muffle this message of love more than strife, competition, and bickering among Christians. The world can look at our apathy, our suspicion, our hostility toward each other, and say, "If that's what you mean by love, I don't want any part of it. That brand of love you call 'divine' is no better than what we call 'human.' "

The church is uniquely loved by Jesus who gave Himself for us. As we uniquely love each other, the message of love is flashed clear and bright in the midst of the world.

Three imperatives flow out of what Jesus has been praying for:

Be the church. That is first. Recognize that you are part of God's people, committed to Him and Jesus Christ whom He has sent. Gather regularly with your brothers and sisters in your appointed place and give thanks to God for the new family He has formed.

In worship bless the name of God for all His works among men. In mission share His name with those who are still strangers to it. In unity, worship and work together to make clear in the midst of life's harrowing insecurities that God is love.

Accept the church. That is the second imperative. It goes without saying that there will be people in any church less attractive than others. There will also be structures of organization, aspects of program, attitudes of ministry to which you are not congenial. But perfection is not the purpose of the church. Worship, fellowship, and mission are. And you'll be surprised how these can go on in less than ideal circumstances.

Take your church as it is, and try to make the best of it. Christ loves all those hard-to-get-along-with people, including you.

Renew the church. That is the third imperative. It reminds us of the words that came out of the Reformation: "the church has been and is ever being re-formed."

In the full sense only God can renew His church. But you and I can be instruments in His hands. We can be obedient to the Scriptures in all they teach about faith and life, and we can encourage others to be the same. As members of the church we can be faithful to our Lord in worship and service, and others will profit from our example.

Many of us are learning to enjoy our oneness in Christ. Not necessarily a oneness of organization or structure, but a oneness that shows itself in a life that is shared, a forgiveness that is experienced, a mission that is pursued, a hope that is enjoyed.

And that's why we go to church.

Here we are before You, Father, Your people with different labels—Presbyterian, Nazarene, Baptist, Pentecostal, Covenant, Methodist, Catholic, Adventist. Let none of the labels permanently divide any whose name You have called to be part of Your church. Let Christian be our highest title because Your forgiveness, purchased on a cross and guaranteed by an empty tomb, has become our richest experience. Through Your holy and divine Son who made us one, we pray. Amen.

WHY WORSHIP?

Pray then like this:

Our Father who art in heaven,
  hallowed be thy name.

Thy kingdom come,
Thy will be done,
  on earth as it is in heaven.
Give us this day our daily bread;
And forgive us our debts,
  as we also have forgiven our debtors;
And lead us not into temptation,
  but deliver us from evil.
For thine is the kingdom,
  and the power,
  and the glory,
  for ever.   Amen.
Matthew 6:9-13

8 WHY WORSHIP?

TO REVERENCE GOD'S PERSON

A lot of people today seem to be down on the church. They feel it doesn't meet their needs. They don't like the music, or they find the sermon dull and boring. Sometimes the members seem a bit cliquish and unfriendly.

So today many Christians are staying home and either ignoring God or worshiping Him on their own. They may meet in small groups for prayer and discussion, but they bypass the church. These are people who can go and don't.

Behind many of the complaints is a basic misunderstanding of our weekly gatherings. Secular ideas creep into our thinking, and worldly standards of efficiency and success are applied.

Why do we go to church?

For the answer to this question we look at the Bible as we do for the solution to all basic questions in life. And a look at the Lord's Prayer may help.

The disciples came to Jesus one day and asked for a prayer that would be their own way of expressing their worship. They wanted a distinct badge which would declare their newfound faith and mark them off from all other religious groups, including the disciples of John the Baptist.

In response to their request, Jesus gave them the Lord's Prayer as the clear expression of their discipleship. Several themes dominate the Lord's Prayer:

First of all, it voices the disciples' *commitment to community.* There is a sense of unity as they say, "Our Father . . . give us this day our daily bread"—not *my* but *our.* It is not that *I* am alone as a disciple, but *we,* who know Christ, are disciples together.

Second, throughout the Prayer there runs the *sense*

of *reverence to God,* a sense of shared reverence. At the beginning we say, "Our Heavenly Father"; we talk about the hallowed, the holy name of God. At the end we address one who is Lord of the kingdom and the power and the glory. From start to finish, we find this mood of reverence.

The result of the stress on reverence is the *confession of dependence* that goes through this Prayer. God alone could sustain the disciples. He alone could forgive them. He alone could deliver them from evil.

Then we shouldn't miss the *spirit of obedience* that runs through the Prayer. The disciples see themselves as subjects of God's kingdom and servants of God's will.

The Lord's Prayer goes to the heart of life. The great issues are spelled out here. The major themes of worship and discipleship are dealt with. The mighty program of God in human history and personal experience is acknowledged and supported, yearned after and longed for.

The glory of God's name and the fulfillment of His will are the disciples' highest ambitions. There is nothing petty, trite, or trivial. The essence of faith and worship are packaged in a paragraph, captured in a capsule.

What can we learn about worship together from the Lord's Prayer?

Worship is central in life. You remember the statement in the old catechism, that man's chief end is to glorify God and to enjoy Him forever. Man was created for the praise of God's glory. Worship is the very staff of human life. Worship is reverence for God's person.

What then does it mean to pray, "Our Father who art in heaven, hallowed be thy name"? We have already seen that Christ gave the Lord's Prayer to His disciples as the hallmark of their discipleship. They were to express their new relationship to God through Jesus Christ in worship. So He taught them to pray, "Our Father who art in heaven, hallowed be thy name."

That's where worship begins, not with requests for God's provision, but with reverence for His person. It is praise to God for who He is.

This is what going to church is all about. God's people gather in Christ's name to worship, to adore, to praise, to celebrate their God and Saviour.

God's Holiness

Our reverence for God is sparked by God's holiness. "Hallowed be thy name." You remember how Job begged for a showdown with God and when God appeared at the end of the book and showed Job what He is really like, Job fell on his face and repented.

You remember how Isaiah (6:1-6) said, "My eyes have seen the King," as he heard the seraphim say, "Holy, holy, holy." Too holy for words is what the repetition implies.

The term holiness means that God is incomparable; it means He is utterly different from us, particularly in righteousness. He is not just like us only a little better; He is so different that contrast, not comparison, is the way to express it.

"I am God, not man," God says in Hosea (11:9), "the Holy One in your midst." That's the difference—a

78

difference not just in size but in essential character.

The name that is hallowed is the expression of God's person, the full manifestation of His character. Juliet may say to Romeo, "What's in a name?" But the Bible answers, there is plenty in a name. God's name reveals His character—a God of might and power, the Lord of salvation and covenant.

This reverence for the name of God is an attitude and experience that we share together. As we salute God's lordly love, we do it as a new people belonging to God, a family, a community. Together we praise God for who He is.

That's why we go to church.

God's Majesty

Our reverence for God is not only sparked by God's holiness but is based on God's majesty. The Father is in *heaven*. Because He is in heaven He has the perspective to see our need. He has insight that we cannot match, a view of reality to which we have no access.

But our Father in heaven not only has a clear perspective to see our need but He has the leverage, the power, to meet our needs. As we are growing up we have the attitude that our fathers can take care of all our problems. We break a toy, scratch a knee, and they take care of the problem. But as time goes by we find there are problems that they can't cope with. This is not so with our heavenly Father. Tragedy, heartbreak, disillusionment, despair—all of these things He has the ability to see and the power to deal with.

As we gather together week by week with the

people of God to worship, we are saying that only God can help us. We are together in our need; we have the same kind of problems, the same kind of limitations. But God is able; He is the heavenly Father, and in the church we bear witness to this together.

God's Fatherhood

But our reverence to God, sparked by God's holiness and based on God's majesty, is enhanced by our intimacy with God. This is a beautiful part of the relationship expressed in the Lord's Prayer. We say "Our Father."

This holy God so different from us, this majestic God in heaven so high above us, we call our Father. It sounds presumptuous; it seems impossible. Yet this is the heart of the gospel. Through Jesus Christ God has become our Father. The Lord of the world has taken us into His family.

Some people say that familiarity breeds contempt, but not with God. The better we know Him, the closer we are to Him, the more we worship Him. He has no flaws; He wears no mask; He never lets us down.

"Dear Father" or "Abba" is what Jesus taught His disciples to call God, and this name speaks of the intimate relationship we have, the rich fellowship that we enjoy with Him. It is a personal relationship but not a private one. We don't possess God; we share Him. To say "Our Father" means that we know Him together, that with other believers we are related to Him.

To say "Our Father" means that we cherish our

intimacy with Him, but also that together as Christians we submit to His authority. He is the heavenly Father, and He asks for our obedience as well as our worship.

As we gather for worship, we rejoice in the new relationship to God and to each other. We salute the person of the God who has called us by name, who has taken us from different families and backgrounds and made us one in Him. We are awed by His holiness; and we are humbled by His majesty; but we are also comforted and encouraged by His fatherhood.

And that's why we go to church.

Three Questions. First, what place does worship have in your life? The mark of discipleship was prayer, a prayer steeped in the reality of worship. Before the disciples worked together in their mission, they prayed together in their worship. They joined the heavens that declare God's glory and the angels who acclaim His holiness. And they said, "Our Father, hallowed be thy name."

Second, do you understand the part that your church plays in your life of worship? Of course worship can be expressed privately, but its chief expression, its clearest form, is in company with others.

God is forming a people, a community. First it was Israel, now it is the church. Worship with the congregation is worship that understands God's purposes. The sermon may not be too good and the music a little out of tune, but when two or three are gathered in Christ's name and around God's Word, the Saviour is present, leading us as we say, "Our Father, hallowed be thy name."

Third, can you really call God "Father"? Do you feel like an outsider at someone else's family reunion? There's nothing private about the Christian faith. Jesus will teach you how to say "Our Father" and to join the band of those who have found life's highest joy in worshiping God. Ask Him to teach you today.

Our Father, what a privilege to call You that! Thank You for not letting Your holiness burn us up by its brightness. Thank You for not letting Your majesty grind us down by its power. Thank You for Your Son, Jesus Christ, who does all things well for You and for us. In His name. Amen.

Pray then like this:
Our Father who are in heaven,
  hallowed be thy name.

Thy kingdom come,
Thy will be done,

  on earth as it is in heaven.
Give us this day our daily bread;
And forgive us our debts,
  as we also have forgiven our debtors;
And lead us not into temptation,
  but deliver us from evil.
For thine is the kingdom,
  and the power,
  and the glory,
  for ever.   Amen.
Matthew 6:9-13

9 WHY WORSHIP?

TO COMMIT OURSELVES TO GOD'S PROGRAM

There's a lot of confusion today about what God is doing in history. Has He backed off from any involvement at all? Is He waiting in the wings for things to get so bad that He will have to break in and straighten them out? Is He just rescuing individuals who call upon Him? Is His purpose to teach us religious knowledge or to call us to prayer?

And what about history itself? Is it standing still while men go their own ways? What is God's plan anyway? What is He doing in the world? And how does the church fit in? What part does my church, the congregation I belong to, have in the plan of God?

This confusion in our attitudes carries over into our view of the church. What is its role? What part does it play in our lives?

For some people, it is the place where they make business contacts. For others, it is an opportunity for social outreach and relationships. Some say the church is the base for community action, the place where they deal with some of the sordid and seedy problems in their neighborhood.

For others, the church is something like a lodge or a club. For some who certainly have deeper insights, the church is the center of spiritual comfort, the place where they enjoy Christian fellowship. And yet in a sense, church is more than any of these.

Earlier we saw the church as the place where God's people gather together to express their reverence for God's person. "Our Father" sounds a note of intimacy made possible through God's Son, Jesus Christ, an intimacy all the more startling in light of God's heavenly majesty and His blazing holiness.

Jesus has given us new access to the person of God, an admirable intimacy with Him. This we celebrate in worship together. Think of it, people from all walks and stations in life gather together to praise their heavenly Father and to salute His holy name. This is what man is made for. This is what life is all about.

Now we carry this a step further and see that worship is not only reverence for God's person, but it is commitment to God's program. Jesus told His disciples, when you pray say, "Thy kingdom come, thy will be done, on earth as it is in heaven." The disciples had asked their Master for a special prayer, their own way of talking to God which would be the badge of their discipleship. Jesus told them to call the God of heaven "Our Father," and to pray that the holiness, the awesome righteousness of this person, would reveal itself in the lives of men.

Look at the close connection between the hallowing of God's name and the coming of God's kingdom. When will God's name really, fully, totally be hallowed? When will men everywhere know that God is God? In the last day, the Bible (Phil. 2:10,11) tells us, at the name of Jesus every knee shall bow and every tongue shall proclaim that Christ is Lord to the glory of God the Father.

The purpose of God's kingdom is to make the holiness, the dignity, the honor, the perfection of God's name known. The coming kingdom means that God's name will be hallowed. Thus we can see how closely tied together are the petitions in this model prayer, this pattern of our discipleship.

Let's look closer at our commitment to God's program. It involves two things: longing for the coming of God's kingdom and committing ourselves to do God's will.

Longing for the Coming of God's Kingdom

The kingdom of God, whose coming we long for as Christians, actually comes in stages. It grows when men are sleeping as Jesus said (Mark 4:26-29). It may start from small beginnings like the mustard seed, but it is God's kingdom and it will grow (Mark 4:30-32).

The Old Testament gives us the picture of preparation for God's kingdom. His saving purposes began to make themselves known as soon as the garden gate clicked closed behind the first man who had revolted against God's rule. In His choice of Abraham He began to call a people who would respect His authority and help restore it among the nations.

Then He set His people free from slavery in Egypt under Moses and set up His rule over them through David the king. But throughout all this Old Testament program the great King was yet to come. The kingdom of God was not yet, though the Old Testament was preparing for it.

Stage one of the kingdom tells us that God's reign has come in Jesus Christ. In Christ we see both the power of the kingdom and the demands of the King.

The Power of the Kingdom. The miraculous setting which surrounded His coming and the wonders He performed throughout His ministry—these are displays of the power of the kingdom.

The angels announced His birth and said, "Peace is coming on earth to men of God's good will." Christ cast out demons; He subdued the storm and controlled nature; He healed the sick who were brought to Him; He made the lame walk and the dead rise; and He preached the gospel to the poor.

In other words, the great enemies of man are controlled by the power of the kingdom, the power and the glory of the age to come. That grand age of God's full sovereignty still lies ahead in history. But its power is already seen in Jesus Christ. The kingdom had come in Him, and He reveals the power of that kingdom.

The Demands of the King. Christ also reveals to us the demands of the King. The kingdom of God was announced by John the Baptist who called men to repent because the kingdom of God was at hand. The kingdom of God involved the renunciation of the ways that we usually go about doing things—wrong, disobedient, rebellious, selfish.

"Repent," John the Baptist said, "and obey the demands of the King because the kingdom is at hand." But repentance is followed by trust, the commitment to take God at His word, the belief that God has acted on our behalf in Jesus Christ, the faith in who Christ is and what He is doing.

The demands of the King are culminated in obedience. He is a king. He demands our allegiance. He wants our will. The kingdom has come in Jesus Christ. That is the first stage. We pray, "Thy kingdom come"; may the fulness of the meaning of the kingdom, the power and the demands of Jesus Christ, be worked out in all of humanity.

Stage two of the kingdom is yet to come in the end times. In other words, the kingdom is here and is still coming. That is the testimony of the New

Testament. Christ is to rule, the apostle Paul says, until He has put all enemies under His feet. Then will He hand the kingdom over to God (1 Cor. 15:24,25).

The kingdoms of the world, these pale reflections, these bent distortions of God's rule, will become the kingdoms of our God and of His Christ. All enemies will be defeated, all wrongs set right; and Christ will reign for ever and ever. That day is yet to come, and what a day it will be.

As we join together to pray, "Thy kingdom come," there is something else we need to see. The kingdom is to be revealed in the lives of God's people. We must submit to God's rule now.

Our prayer, "Thy kingdom come," has to be matched by our willingness to be obedient subjects of the King. To His people God has committed the message of His rule. When we worship together we commit ourselves to the program that God is working out in history, the program which gives life and history their meaning.

And that's why we go to church.

Commitment to the Doing of God's Will

When we do go to church we pray, "Thy kingdom come." The commitment to God's program not only involves longing for the coming of God's kingdom, it involves the doing of God's will. We take this as a further explanation of the meaning of God's kingdom.

Doing God's will brings a unity to life that glues our words and deeds together. I suppose that knowing what we should do is one of the hardest chores of life. We are surrounded by advice; we are torn by competing choices. We rashly rush into a wrong decision, or we stew in apathy and lose ourselves by hesitation.

Doing God's will can wrap our living up in a package that can stand the wear and tear of hectic circumstances. Who knows better what is good for us than God who made us? Doing the will of God gives us unprecedented freedom.

At first glance we might be tempted to think of it as restricting or confining; but it is freeing; it is liberating. There's no need for us to mince our way nervously, to pick our steps along the ledges of life edgily.

We can walk free and bold, guided by God's will, protected from our foolishness by His direction. Together as members of the church of Christ we have found that God's will is best, and we commit ourselves to His program.

And that's why we go to church and pray, "Thy kingdom come, they will be done."

The gist of what I am saying is this: we go to church because we are not spectators but participants in the program of God. The greatest drama in life is going on in the church of Jesus Christ. God is working out a saving mission in the world, and strange as it may seem, is using the church to do it. He who chose a struggling nation in the Old Testament and then sent His Son to be a carpenter is using you and your church to make His name known throughout the world.

When we go to church we are not rebels or shirkers, not idle hearers, but we are doers of God's will.

Obedience is what God desires. His Father love deserves it; His holiness demands it; His kingship requires it. So let's get on with it.

"Who are My mother and My brothers?" Jesus Christ once asked. "Whoever does the will of God is my brother, and sister, and mother" (Mark 3:33,34).

Relax in the will of God. Submit to Christ's kingly claims. Commit yourself to God's saving program. Get in tune with the symphony of history which God Himself is conducting.

Our Father, Thy kingdom come, Thy will be done. Through Your Son, we pray. Amen.

Pray then like this:
Our Father who art in heaven,
  hallowed be thy name.
Thy kingdom come,
Thy will be done,
  on earth as it is in heaven.

Give us this day our daily bread;

And forgive us our debts,
  as we also have forgiven our debtors;
And lead us not into temptation,
  but deliver us from evil.
For thine is the kingdom,
  and the power,
  and the glory,
  for ever.   Amen.
Matthew 6:9-13

10 WHY WORSHIP?

TO ACKNOWLEDGE OUR DEPENDENCE ON GOD

Did it ever strike you as surprising that "bread" is mentioned in the middle of the Lord's Prayer? How does something so mundane fit in among the high and lofty ideas we have seen?

We have talked about the holy name of God, the wonder and power of the kingdom that has come and is yet to come, the sovereignty of God's royal will done so perfectly in heaven and so imperfectly on earth, the beautiful intimacy of our sonship where we call God, the God of the universe, our Father. Yet in the midst of all this there is the mention of bread.

I personally think that it is a good place to talk about bread and that bread is a good thing to have in the center of our asking. Let's try to see why.

We have been asking the question, "Why go to church?" This is not just an academic or theoretical query. A lot of people are asking it, and a lot of people have already answered it by not going. Then there are some, maybe you are among them, who go regularly and faithfully and yet don't really know why.

The point of the Lord's Prayer is that Jesus has called us to be His disciples and has put worship, not just private devotion, but public worship, at the heart of our discipleship. There is a built-in togetherness to God's program in history. He's forming a people to praise His name. Christ's body is *one*.

And there's a built-in togetherness to our response to that program. As His people we gather regularly to celebrate His lordship, to remember the holiness of His name and our oneness as children of the heavenly Father. He who taught us to let God's name be hallowed, to pray for the coming of the kingdom, and to bend to His will, also commands us to ask for bread.

This is a crucial part of our worship. Worship is not only reverence for God's person, not only commitment to God's program, but it is also an acknowledgment of His provision and our complete and constant dependence upon Him.

God's Care Is for Daily Living

When we pray, "Give us this day our daily bread," we are talking about God's care in the midst of our daily living. You'll note that it is necessities, not luxuries, that He is talking about. We know the importance of bread. In both ancient and modern times it has often been called "the staff of life."

I suppose you could say that bread is a good way of packaging and preserving the nourishment of grain. It keeps well; it is easy to carry; it is fairly simple to make.

One of the old Middle Eastern poets talked about "a loaf of bread, a jug of wine and thou"—the combination of nourishment, refreshment, and companionship—as the essence of life.

God in His abundant grace, in His lavish care of us, may go far beyond bread; but our prayer is not for what might come but what we really need. "Give us this day our daily bread." This request is no less necessary in our modern age than it was in days gone by.

Whether we know it or not, we are just as dependent on God now as we ever were. That is hard for us to come to grips with, for we have freezers full of meat, canned juice, vegetables; we have cupboards and larders full of cans and packages; we have a supermarket a five-minute walk away. And yet we must pray, "Give us this day our daily bread."

The thing we have to remember is that God is the God of the quick freeze. He is the Lord of the vacuum pack. He is in charge of the dehydrating processes that preserve food. You who live on farms will know that God is God of hybrid seeds and automated silage.

After all, who *is* responsible for the laws of nature that make preserving and packaging possible? Man in our modern world has only found out how to harness the principles that God built into the stuff of reality from the beginning.

It is good to remember that our God, the God of the Bible, is not a God of the gap. He is not a God whom we bring in just to explain the mysteries of life. He is not a God who is withdrawn from everyday occurrences. Only He can really cause things to grow. No one else that you know, or ever will know, has power to create.

Even our scientists who are doing such magnificent things are only rearranging elements that God has made. In the midst of our modern age with all of our technology and all of our conveniences, we will still pray day after day after day, "Give us this day our daily bread." And if God's grace were ever to be withheld, we would know how heavily we depend upon Him.

God's Care Comes in Community

There is another point to see in God's care for

our daily lives: it usually comes to us in community. Did you ever think of how many people were involved in the preparation of that head of lettuce that you buy in the market? There is the farmer with all the people who supply the chemicals, the fertilizers, and the seeds to him. There are the pickers, the truckers, the packers, the people at the wholesale market, the retail buyer who goes down early in the morning to get that lettuce, the produce trimmer who gets it in shape to put on the stand, the checker who charges you for it, and the boy who carries it out in the bag with your other groceries.

Behind each loaf of bread there is the same kind of group. In other words, we're not individuals directly fed by God. When we pray, "Give us this day our daily bread," we are acknowledging that God may bring that daily bread to us with the help of a great many other people who are bound up in the bundle of life and society with us.

When we get together to worship in church, we are acknowledging our dependence on God and on each other. God uses people to minister to our needs, and He also marks off a group to respond together to His goodness.

We ought to remember too the obligation we have to use our abundance, to share our surplus. God may use us to answer the prayers of others who pray, "Give us this day our daily bread." Part of our gathering to worship is the recognition that God has called us together as a community to take care of each other's needs.

And that is why we go to church.

God's Care Is for Total Need

There is something else involved in this text that we have to see: God's total care of all of our needs, not just physical needs. God is committed to us totally. Bread is a symbol of spiritual sustenance. There was shewbread in the Tabernacle, symbolic of God's constant provision. And Christ calls Himself the Bread of Life given for the needs of the world.

The phrase that we translate "our daily bread" may also be translated "bread of tomorrow." The Greek word here is a little difficult and only occurs once in the New Testament. When all the possibilities are weighed, it may mean that we are asking for tomorrow's bread today. Just enough bread, in other words, to tide us over.

And yet at the same time, since so much of the Lord's Prayer looks to the future, we may see in this petition for bread a longing for the time when we will feed to the full on Jesus Christ who is the Bread of Life, the time when we will share Christ's glory and be completely sustained and nourished by Him.

Until then the Word of God, which is also the Bread of Life, keeps us going. We are strengthened as God speaks. Muscle is built; fibers are fed; our will to do His will is renewed. Our love, so easily depleted, is given fresh supply. And this is essential.

We as human beings may act like animals sometimes and forget we have spiritual needs. At five o'clock our dogs are desperate to be fed, but they don't have many other needs that they are conscious of. Pet them a little and play with them some. That is all.

But we are not dogs; we are persons. We are made

to be sustained by fellowship with God. And we are as helpless without Him as an astronaut without oxygen. When we go to church together, we hear the living Word and our life is renewed. It comes to us as bread to the hungry.

And that is why we go to church.

In the middle of the prayer, bread. I am reminded of the time I came to the end of a busy day of meetings, saw a note on my desk and thought, "This must be an important phone call, a crucial message." The note said, "Can you pick up two quarts of milk and a loaf of bread on the way home?" An important message it was.

God is never too busy to be involved in our daily needs, and He reminds us that our nagging present concerns are on His mind. Our daily lives are of importance to Him. His kingdom, His power, His glory are crucial; but so is our bread—both physical and spiritual. God's care binds these two realms together intimately into one in Himself. He ministers to both our physical and spiritual needs. He wants it that way.

God's commitment to us penetrates every area of our lives. Because He is our heavenly Father, we can think of Him and think of bread at the same time. No area of our lives is marked off from Him. The menial, the trivial, the mundane are familiar terrain to Him.

The Lord of the universe is at home in our offices, our workshops, our classrooms, and our kitchens. We can pray, "Give us our daily bread." And yet He knows the total needs of man. He knows that bread is not enough. He knows we need more than bread—

His words, His love, His life itself. And He offers these through His Son.

As you eat your meals today, thank God. As you plan your menu for tomorrow, pray for your daily bread but do more than this: hunger and thirst after God's righteousness and ask God to fill you. He has more than enough bread, both physical and spiritual, to meet all of your needs.

Our Father, who art in heaven, hallowed be Thy name. Give us this day our bread for tomorrow and teach us to share it with others. Nourish us totally; feed us to the full. For Jesus' sake. Amen.

Pray then like this:
Our Father who art in heaven,
hallowed be thy name.
Thy kingdom come,
Thy will be done,
on earth as it is in heaven.
Give us this day our daily bread;

And forgive us our debts,
as we also have forgiven our debtors;

And lead us not into temptation,
but deliver us from evil.
For thine is the kingdom,
and the power,
and the glory,
for ever.   Amen.
Matthew 6:9-13

TO CONFESS
OUR SIN

You open the mail, and all you get are bills. Bills and more bills pile up on the desk or sideboard until you can barely see over them. Someone once told me that she owed so much money to so many people that she couldn't even answer the phone. She was sure it would be one of her creditors hounding her for money.

It is a terrible thing to be in debt. Some people have to borrow more money to pay off what they already owe. An endless cycle as the old song says, "Another day older and deeper in debt."

Not all of us are in this kind of situation. Some of you have managed your affairs quite well, and others of you have been blessed with means enough to keep out of debt. Yet, when it comes right down to it, we are all in debt. The Bible tells us we are in debt to God, and we want to see what that means.

We are grappling with the question, "Why go to church?" and are using the Lord's Prayer as our pattern. So what do we mean when we pray, "Forgive us our debts, as we forgive our debtors?" Debt is also described as sin. In the account of the Lord's Prayer that Luke (11:4) gives us, the word "sin" is used. But Matthew (6:12) uses a term that would be readily understood by Jesus' disciples, because the Jews in Jesus' time often described *sin* as *debt*. That is a good way to put it when it comes right down to it.

The Nature of Our Debts

We see two things here: the nature of our debts and the importance of our response. Now, as to the nature of our debts, they are primarily owed to God.

God made us and He made us for a purpose. He has given us all that we have in this world of ours to help us fulfill this purpose.

For us to fail in our obligation to cooperate with God's purposes and to do His will is to pile up debt. It is to create a backlog of unpaid obligations. In other words, it is to be in the hole as far as God is concerned; it is to owe God plenty and not be able to work our way out.

Now let's suppose a wealthy man came along and gave to us a large amount of money for the specific purpose of guarding it, investing it, using it for him. Instead we lose it in gambling game, or we walk by a fine clothing store and squander the money on fancy clothes. Embezzling is what we call this. We owe the person the money, and we may go to prison for the crime.

God says we should seek forgiveness for our debts, our failures to be what God made us to be. Let's not bog down here in minor issues or get tied up in nit-picking. Our basic failures are so large that we should not allow ourselves to be distracted by undue attention to lesser items. I am not saying these things are not important at all; I am just saying they're not as crucial or central as some of the things I want to talk about.

To put it bluntly our sin, our debt, is failure to come to grips with the spirit of the first petitions in the Lord's Prayer. The Lord's Prayer not only tells us how we should worship, but it serves as a guide to show us how we have failed. Have we hallowed God's name? Do we long for His kingdom to come? Have we bent ourselves to do His will?

These are basic questions that none of us can shy away from. They strike at the heart of our humanity and lay bare our failures. We may try to rationalize by saying we aren't as bad as we could be, or that we are better than someone else we know.

But these excuses won't hold water when we measure ourselves by God's standards. All we can do is ask for forgiveness. When we gather together at church, this is just what we are doing.

Our neighbors may think the world owes them a living, that the human family is lucky to have them as members. But you and I know that the obligation runs the other way. Life itself is a gift to be cherished and used for high and holy purposes. We know that we are God's debtors and live by His forgiveness, if we live at all.

And that is why we go to church.

The Importance of Our Response

We see not only the nature of our debts, but we have to look at the importance of our response as given to us in the Lord's Prayer. The text says not only, "Forgive us our debts," but goes on to say, "as we forgive our debtors." If you notice the order of the statements, God's forgiveness has the priority over ours.

God's forgiveness comes first and then ours, because *He is the true judge of sin*. We have a hard time telling right from wrong. He alone knows for sure. We can't read our own hearts let alone the hearts of anyone else, so we have to ask God to forgive us. He shows us how we have sinned against Him, before we can begin to exercise the kind of forgiveness we want toward others.

God's forgiveness has the priority because *sin is directed against Him.* As the creator of the world and the maker of man, God has most at stake in our sin. Whatever we do wrong touches Him. He made us and loves us, so when we hurt ourselves, He is concerned; any marring of His children or malice toward His creatures touches Him, even when the connection is not clear to us.

God's forgiveness has the priority because *our forgiveness is learned from Him.* You and I learn to forgive by being forgiven. Now this learning probably starts in our homes. Some parents make a terrible fuss when their youngsters make mistakes. Milk is spilled, and there is a lot of crying about it despite the wisdom of the proverb. When a child wants to do something, old wrongs are often thrown in his face. Parents who ought to forgive and forget keep reminding their youngsters, and the youngsters grow up to be harsh, bitter, unforgiving.

Our forgiveness is best shown in a community relationship. The church gives us a marvelous opportunity to express forgiveness, for there we gather with people from all kinds of backgrounds, people we may be attracted to and people we don't quite like.

And yet, when we have been forgiven by God, we learn to accept each other; and that is one of the reasons we go to church—to show the meaning of God's forgiveness.

When we promise to forgive as God forgives us, we are not bargaining with God, we are not saying that His forgiveness is meted out to us in the measure that we manage to eke out forgiveness for others. This would be a dreary picture. Our forgiveness is our pale, our limping response to what God has already done so fully and freely for us.

His forgiveness is lavish, not grudging. He longs to forgive those who call upon Him. Our forgiveness of our debtors is meant to show that we have really grasped the meaning of God's grace. The light has been turned on; we now understand the forgiveness that is the law of life. By forgiving others we share this understanding.

The Lord's Prayer has an eye on the future. It longs for the day when the holiness of God's name will be recognized. It anticipates with rapid pulse the hour when God's will becomes the norm and standard for all men. It hints of the bread of life, the bread of tomorrow, on which God's people will feed to the full when they sit down with their Saviour at the marriage supper of the Lamb.

The mention of forgiveness also takes us into the future. It reminds us that judgment lies ahead if there is not forgiveness, and it reminds us that forgiveness is possible because Christ has borne our judgment. But Jesus' mention of forgiveness in the Lord's Prayer also announces that the time of the new covenant, the time of God's great future, has already arrived.

It was Jeremiah, you will recall, who foresaw a time when the law would be written on the hearts of God's people. "I will forgive their iniquity, and I will remember their sin no more," is what God promised (Jer. 31:34).

Forgiveness is a mark, perhaps the key mark of the new covenant. And in the Lord's Prayer Jesus is saying that this new age has come; the Messiah is here. Full forgiveness is possible.

Judgment day need hold no terror because Christ has taken its full force in our place. The whole weight of judgment has fallen on Him and need not descend on us. God stands ready to forgive, and to forgive *you.*

Our Father, we confess that without Your forgiveness we can't really live. We rejoice in the freedom that the new life of Jesus Christ has brought about—the freedom from judgment and condemnation. And we pray that You'll help us to understand it better and to live in its fulness here and now. Through Jesus Christ our Lord. Amen.

Pray then like this:
Our Father who art in heaven,
hallowed be thy name.
Thy kingdom come,
Thy will be done,
on earth as it is in heaven.
Give us this day our daily bread;
And forgive us our debts,
as we also have forgiven our debtors;

And lead us not into temptation,
but deliver us from evil.

For thine is the kingdom,
and the power,
and the glory,
for ever.   Amen.
Matthew 6:9-13

TO PRAY
FOR POWER

Temptation is one of the sure marks of our humanity. It's an experience that ties us all together. We human beings are a motley bunch in many ways. Ever sit in an airport or a bus station and watch different people? We come in all colors, shapes and sizes. We are all as different as our fingerprints attest.

Yet one of the chief experiences we have in common is temptation. It doesn't matter where you are in the world today; it doesn't matter what your walk or station in life may be. You know about temptation, and you know about it firsthand. We have temptation in common; it is deeply rooted in our humanity.

The first man, Adam, was tempted in the garden. Before the Fall, before that grave and awful disobedience, there was temptation. You can imagine the many times Adam strolled through the garden and said to himself, "Why do I have access to all the other trees and not this one?"

Then the last man, Jesus Christ, was tempted not in the garden but in a wilderness. His full identification with our humanity is stressed here. He became our complete representative before God. Temptation has touched the first man and the last man and every one else in between.

As needful as our daily bread, which was in the center of the Lord's Prayer, is power to face temptation. So Christ commanded us to pray, "Lead us not into temptation, but deliver us from evil."

The Need for Power

Two points we want to make: the need for power and the supply of power. We need power in coping with temptation. Connect this with the petition that

114

comes in the Lord's Prayer just before it. The offer of forgiveness without the power to cope with temptation might lead to terrible abuse.

We could say to ourselves, "Just give in blandly to temptation and then ask heartily for forgiveness." The sequence of the petitions is important. There will be no power without forgiveness, but forgiveness should not lead us to license.

We cannot supply our own bread; we cannot forgive our own sin; and we cannot handle temptation in our strength. We seek God's help.

The phrase, "Lead us not," means "Don't let us come into the grips of temptation so that it will get us down; don't let us yield to it or collapse in the midst of it." The word "temptation" could be translated "trial" or "test." "Do not test us beyond what we can take; do not let us flunk the great test."

Notice that I put emphasis on *the great temptation,* the temptation to give up our faith, to fail to worship God, to sell out our trust in His plan in history and in His will for our lives. It is a temptation in basic allegiance that Jesus had in view. Other temptations may strengthen us and we can rejoice in them, as James told us (James 1:2-4).

Life without temptation of any kind would be boring. It is part of our humanity that we are toughened and strengthened by temptation. What Jesus is telling us deals with the great test in life, not with some of the other lesser temptations that come along the way.

And this great test is connected with the attempt of the evil one to gain mastery over our lives. That is why this petition, "Lead us not into temptation," is followed immediately by the statement, "but deliver us from evil."

Behind the temptation stands the tempter, as in the garden with Adam and in the wilderness with Jesus Christ. We have to be at the ready to deal with the tempter's presence and power.

You know the many forms in which he comes, but his master plan is always the same: to get us to renounce the worship of God. That was his aim in the beginning, and that was what he tried with Jesus Christ.

He wants us to shun the worship of God and to serve our own purposes, which is to serve his. "Deliver us from the evil *one,*" we pray. Evil, here, is not just a vague influence, but an active enemy setting traps for us continually, luring us into arrogance, into insolence, into unfaithfulness or idolatry.

Our Lord Jesus Christ took the existence of Satan seriously, and He told us to ask God to rescue us from him. We ought to do just that. Sometimes in the midst of our super-sophistication in the modern age we have the feeling that references to the devil are rather old-fashioned, and this is exactly what the devil wants us to believe. To ignore the evil one is to play into his hands.

But the opposite is true. To doubt that God will rescue and deliver us is to surrender without a fight. In facing the great tests in life, we have to admit that we need help and then claim God's help. Part of our worshiping together, part of our going to church, is to confess that we cannot make it on our own and to humbly seek God's strength.

And that is why we go to church.

The Supply of Power

Not only do we want to recognize our need for power, the power to cope with temptation from the evil one, but also we want to rejoice in the supply of power that God makes available. As in all the other petitions, Christ Himself is the one who provides the answer. The promise of supply is included in the commands to pray.

Earthly fathers don't ordinarily tease their youngsters by holding up standards impossible for them to fulfill. We don't give stones, Jesus said, when we're asked for bread, or scorpions when a fish is requested. We want to help our children all we can. (See Matt. 7:9-11.)

And how much more does our heavenly Father care for us? (See Luke 11:11-13.) The purpose of this prayer is not to baffle us or to frustrate us, but to show us what to ask for and to assure us that God Himself will provide the answer. And His answer comes through Jesus Christ.

Notice the connection between the petitions which Jesus had been teaching His disciples and the long temptation in the wilderness where the evil one put Him to the test. In other words, when Jesus instructs us in prayer, He mentions experiences which He himself has tasted.

When He told us to ask for daily bread, He knew the hunger of forty days without bread. When He urges us to pray, "Lead us not into temptation," He knew what it was to be put to the test not once but three times.

He was tested on all points, the author of Hebrews tells us, yet without sin (Heb. 4:15). And He certainly knew the power of the evil one. He had met him head on and defeated him.

This side of the cross and resurrection we know even more of Christ's power. Satan tried his best to do Him in, but the Saviour was more than a match for him. From Christ's victory we can gain strength for ours. Our leader is a winner, the Bible says, and we can trust Him to see us through.

It may well be that one of the ways in which we can gain strength for temptation is through the encouragement of other Christians. Alcoholics Anonymous and Weight Watchers have taught us a lot about our need for help from each other. There are lots of areas where mutual strength and comfort should be given by fellow Christians. We cannot fight the tempter alone; we need each other.

If we cannot find love and sympathy in the church, where do we find it? We are all sinners there, and no one can pull rank. I suppose you could call members of the church Sinners Anonymous. Grace is our only hope; forgiveness is all we can count on. God's strength is all we have. Remember what Luther's old hymn says, "Did we in our own strength confide, our striving would be losing."

We take comfort in the mutual support that comes from knowing we belong to Christ together. No one can look down on anyone else because we are all tempted. No one is better than anyone else because we are all bound to God by forgiveness alone.

Together we confess our complete dependence on God. "Hangs my helpless soul on thee" is what we sing. Together we receive the news that Satan is doomed and Christ is victor. Together we rejoice in that news and give thanks.

And that is why we go to church.

We go to church not just to gain information from the teaching, although I would be the last one to knock the importance of information. It is not just the music we go to enjoy (sometimes the choir is better than other times); it is not the architecture or the stained glass.

We go to worship God, and we go to do this not just as individuals but as the people of God, the company that God Himself is forming. We are part of the new humanity that God is bringing about in Jesus Christ.

As Peter puts it, we are a nation, a race, a priesthood, a people (1 Pet. 2:9). God is saving a community and using that community to make His saving program known. By gathering together, we draw strength from the group, from Christ's body in whom His Spirit dwells; we gain grace to stand tall in the great temptations of life, grace to resist the lure of the evil one, bucked up by the knowledge that Christ and His people will conquer.

Going to church is important. It shows that we know what God is doing and are a part of it. It shows that we know how heavily, how totally, we depend on Him. And we want to do that regularly.

Don't vote against church by apathy and absence. If you belong to God the heavenly Father through His Son, you belong to God's people as well. Join with them regularly; rejoice in Christ's victory over all our enemies; and gain strength from that rejoicing to conquer temptation and to frustrate the tempter.

We thank you, Father, that with the command to resist temptation is also the power for this resistance and the promise that victory is assured in Jesus Christ. Help us to live in the strength and the glory of that victory. Through Christ the Lord victorious, we pray. Amen.

Pray then like this:
Our Father who art in heaven,
  hallowed be thy name.
Thy kingdom come,
Thy will be done,
  on earth as it is in heaven.
Give us this day our daily bread;
And forgive us our debts,
  as we also have forgiven our debtors;
And lead us not into temptation,
  but deliver us from evil.

For thine is the kingdom,
  and the power,
  and the glory,

  for ever.   Amen.
Matthew 6:9-13

13 WHY WORSHIP?

TO DECLARE OUR HOPE AND DESTINY

The tension between what we hear in church and what we read in the newspaper is a real one. In church we hear that "the earth is the Lord's and everything that fills it" (Ps. 24:1), and in the newspaper we read about the mounting statistics of crime, national and international unrest, immorality, apathy. How different is the world as we see it in the news from what the Lord wants it to be.

And yet our confession that to the Lord belongs "the kingdom and the power and the glory," is more true than anything we read in the headlines. We have an illustration here, when we see the contrast between what we affirm in church and what we hear in the news, of the truth of Paul's statement: "The things that are seen are transient, but the things that are unseen are eternal" (2 Cor. 4:18).

We have noticed the two bright ideas that shine through the Lord's Prayer: God is completely sovereign; and we are totally dependent upon Him. As we gather in church with the people of God to worship Him, we acknowledge His sovereignty. His name is hallowed. That is, He is different from anyone else. He is distinct, unique, and holy, the only one in all of the universe worthy of our worship.

Man can worship God alone without degrading himself because man is more important than anything else in the whole wide universe save God himself. We acknowledge God's sovereignty by talking about His kingdom and His will, which alone will bring order out of the spiritual confusion in which we stew. No man-made program can do it.

And as we gather in church with the people of God, we confess not only His sovereignty but our dependence on Him. The human body cannot sustain itself. We are totally dependent on resources outside of ourselves. And where do they come from? From God, of course.

We are dependent on God for sins forgiven. There is no spiritual eraser with which we can rub out the past. Man has no power to revive himself. Only God can forgive. Only God can make alive. We are dependent on God for deliverance from the testings of the evil one. There is no iron in the human will that cannot be bent to wrong purposes unless God helps. We need His stiffness and His strength, the courage and the conviction that His presence brings to us.

We are creatures, needy and helpless, and we are sinners, rebellious and bitter. We are waifs, lost and lonely, but God invites us to say, "Our Father." He calls us to put our hands in His, to lift our eyes to Him, and to revel in His grace.

Hope in God's Program

It is then that our worship of God becomes an affirmation of hope and destiny. We have hope in God's program and so we pray, "Thine is the kingdom."

Think of all the false hopes that are raised by other kingdoms, kingdoms that come and go. The paths of history are strewn with the wrecks of political structures that have promised more than they can produce. They have promised peace and order and security, and they have often resulted in slavery and oppression and hardship.

Some kingdoms are better than others, and some

systems of life are better than others; but none can adequately deal with the human heart; none really knows what is wrong with human life. They are all stamped by the Fall. Their rulers are all human beings.

But the Lord's Prayer tells us God is at work. He has caught us up in the program that He has planned for all eternity. We participate in it. We not only pray for the kingdom, but we are part of it as we commit ourselves to faith in and obedience to Jesus Christ.

And that is why we go to church.

Hope in God's Power

"Thine is the power," we say. Think of man's use of power: economic power which may be used to bless and to help people also can be used to increase the wealth of the wicked or ambitious; political power which should keep law and order, which is meant to solve human problems and to organize human resources, often can go sour; intellectual power which seeks to unfold the mysteries of the universe, to unwrap the secrets of life and study the past, and to discern the trends of the future, can lead us astray.

Someone once pointed out that if you have a little boy who steals rides on the bus line, and you give him the wrong kind of education without training him morally and spiritually, he may grow up to be a crook and by graft steal the whole transportation system.

Only God can bend the will for good, only God can renew the human spirit when it is bogged down

126

in guilt and frustration and uncertainty. Only God can plan right and then carry out His plans.

Maybe you saw a cartoon that pictured a designer watching while his airplane was being tested. Before his eyes the airplane went into a spin, stalled, and crashed. He wiped his hands and turned away muttering, "Back to the old drawing board."

And so it is with most of our plans, but not with God's. It is our privilege to draw on God's power, and it is our responsibility to celebrate God's power.

And that is why we go to church.

Hope in God's Purpose

"Thine is the glory," we pray. Our lives are paralyzed by lack of goals, partly because there seem to be so many choices. Our front doors are picketed by a dozen placards which invite us to lose ourselves in various causes.

"Make money; that's the key to life."

"Enjoy yourself; life is short."

"Study hard; learning brings prestige."

"Just relax; most problems will go away by themselves anyhow."

In the midst of this swirl of advice, the Christian faith says: "Glorify God and enjoy Him forever." This is why God created man in the first place—to have a people made in His image, revealing His glory, spelling out His love, serving His purposes and His program. His kingdom is geared to do just that. And He has the power to implement His program.

See how these three great words in the Lord's Prayer fit together and form a pattern. God's purpose is to make His glory known. The way He does this is to establish a kingdom; that is, He rules the hearts and lives of His people; and He has the power to make this rule complete, to carry it out to the last detail.

And so the Lord's Prayer rings with hope. It is alive with certainty. Our requests are being answered. The success of God's program is not in doubt for a moment, no matter what the headlines may say.

And that is why we go to church.

Our confidence and our hope that we express as we gather together to worship are underscored by the victories that Jesus Christ has already won. Take His temptation for example. He taught us some important lessons here. You remember that Christ was offered the kingdoms of earth, but He knew that God was the real owner of these kingdoms, and God's program was to give these kingdoms to Him in another way—through His cross and not through false worship.

We not only learn lessons about God's program from the temptations of Christ, but about God's power. You remember that Christ was challenged to turn stones into bread. But the purpose of God's power is not flashy display or even physical ministry. Rather it is to carry out God's program of making His splendor, His glory known. Spiritual priorities outrank physical, as important as the physical may be.

And then God's purpose is mentioned in the temptation story. Christ was tempted to use God's glory for selfish, showy purposes, jumping from the pinnacle of the Temple and daring God to rescue Him. But God's purpose is not to stage a show. He is not

Barnum and Bailey. Carnivals and circuses are not His business. He wants people who love and worship Him, who reveal His glory not in the spectacular, but in the ordinary life of worship and loving service.

By resisting the false, by rejecting the counterfeit, Christ paved the way for the true kingdom, the right use of power, the lasting display of God's glory. We can be thankful that He did, because now we can shout with unbounded certainty, "Thine is the kingdom, and the power, and the glory."

I need to say a word to you who are pastors. As you lead your people in worship week after week, let the Lord's Prayer set the pattern. Lead the people of God in the worship of God. Don't hammer or harangue, attack or defend, but lift your hearts and theirs to worship, to adore, and to pray for specific needs, and then to receive the assurance of forgiveness, of provision, of power.

Remember that these people whom you lead in worship are the people of the kingdom, the power, and the glory. Now I know that we don't always look like it or act like it, but the people who have trusted Jesus Christ as Saviour are the ones through whom God is making His name known. Take heart in rough times and hard places. God is at work and He can't fail.

Some of you young people should consider the church as the place to spend your life and your ministry. It may seem dead and dull at times, and its people may lack luster; but the church is where the action is. God's action.

He has taken the risk of choosing the church and using it to fulfill His mission. Other institutions may look more appealing and seem to have greater stability, but God is counting on the church to work out His will in history. Where better can you spend your lives than ministering among the people of God in the program that God Himself is working out to His glory?

Thank you, Father, for telling us about Yourself, for letting us get to know Your kingdom, which lasts forever, Your power equal to any task, and Your glory, which knows no rival. And thank You for Your church. Help us to be faithful to You as part of it. Through Jesus Christ our Lord. Amen.

LET'S WORSHIP?

Come to him, to that living stone, rejected by men but in God's sight chosen and precious; and like living stones be yourselves built into a spiritual house, to be a holy priesthood, to offer spiritual sacrifices acceptable to God through Jesus Christ.

For it stands in scripture:

"Behold, I am laying in Zion a stone, a cornerstone chosen and precious, and he who believes in him will not be put to shame."

To you therefore who believe, he is precious, but for those who do not believe,

"The very stone which the builders rejected has become the head of the corner," and

"A stone that will make men stumble, a rock that will make them fall"; for they stumble because they disobey the word, as they were destined to do.

But you are a chosen race, a royal priesthood, a holy nation, God's own people, that you may declare the wonderful deeds of him who called you out of darkness into his marvelous light.

Once you were no people but now you are God's people; once you had not received mercy but now you have received mercy.

1 Peter 2:4-10

SEE YOU
IN CHURCH

Sometimes I feel like this is where I came in. I feel that way when I look at the church of Jesus Christ. As a boy in the 1930s, I knew the meaning of the *old fundamentalism*—as part and parcel of it, stamped in a great many ways by its strengths and weaknesses. As a young man in the forties, I tried to wrestle through the meaning of my own faith in college and the beginning of seminary. In the 1950s, as graduate student and teacher, I began to see more and more what the church of Jesus Christ really is; and as minister and theological educator in the sixties, I continued to wrestle with the question of the church.

As I look at the church at the beginning of the seventies, I sometimes feel that this is where I came in. We are confronted with a *new fundamentalism*.

The old fundamentalism had some magnificent fruits: its commitment to the authority of Scripture and the other basics of our faith, its recognition of the perils of the old liberalism, its zeal for evangelism and mission, its concern for a biblical education (particularly in the movement of Bible schools and Bible conferences). But it failed to find a mature doctrine of the church.

A new fundamentalism will also make some outstanding contributions with its emphasis on relationships; on open, earnest communication; on our commitment to each other as persons. But it, too, may slip into the same pitfalls when it comes to the doctrine of the church.

The old fundamentalism said, "I will only worship comfortably, I will only align myself fully with those who are correct in their propositions doctrinally."

The new fundamentalism says, "I will only feel

at home as a Christian with those who are sound in their vibrations emotionally."

So what we are facing now I would call a *psychic sectarianism.* This itself is a move beyond the private faith which characterized so much of the old fundamentalism—a faith that said, "If I have my propositions right, if I know Jesus Christ is my personal Saviour, if I have been through the experience of a new birth, then everything else is settled. My ultimate destiny in heaven is assured, and what I do between now and then will largely be to keep myself as pure as I can within the pagan contexts where I live."

We have now gone beyond that private faith to an emphasis on group fellowship and on group relationship which has some beautiful facets to it. But both fundamentalisms, the old and the new, suffer from a futile quest for a pure church.

It was doctrinal purity in the old fundamentalism. It is emotional compatibility in the new fundamentalism. Both expressions of fundamentalism need to look afresh at what Scripture teaches about the church. Peter's first letter at chapter 2 helps us do just that.

Not Groups, but a People

The first aspect of Peter's doctrine of the church is that it is not groups, but a people.

Groups as a complementary and auxiliary style of Christian gathering have a magnificent role in encouragement, in nurture, in prayer, in planning for mission. They allow us to be ourselves and to be affirmed in a situation where we are accepted and appreciated. This is a rich experience. It means a great deal to me any time I find myself as part of that kind of group. But the spirit of the new fundamentalism takes over when that group becomes for us a substitute for the gathered congregation.

Because what God is doing is not calling little groups here and there, but forming one people. Even college chapel services are not a substitute, as desirable as they are; they are not the ultimate expression of the people of God because there are those who are excluded by the very nature of academic affiliation. To be worshiping in a chapel service, one needs to be part of an academic community—teaching, serving as a member of the staff, student body, or a visitor with special credentials that allow him to feel at home in an academic context.

Where doctors meet for prayer on Wednesday afternoon, or school teachers on a Thursday morning, where students gather in dormitories on Friday nights after the basketball game or young couples meet in homes for Bible study, there you have expressions of the people of God. But you do not really have the church, because you do not have the cross-section of society that gathers when a congregation meets for worship.

This cross-section is the essence of the church: the secret that God is working out in history is that a people is being formed—a people who may have nothing in common, except the grace of God that has worked in their lives through Jesus Christ. The spirit of the new fundamentalism says, "But I feel more *comfortable* in a small group," and, of course, we do with our peers, with people with whom we have ready acceptance, instant identification.

But that is not the purpose of gathered worship. By God's grace we may be comforted, but He has not promised to make us feel comfortable. *So it is not groups, but a people that God is forming.*

Note the language that the apostle uses as he sums up his great doctrine of the church: a "race," a "priesthood," a "nation," a "people." These generic terms, these massive terms, these broad, all-inclusive terms picture God moving through the course of history and through the family of men and reaching out into every age group and every cultural sector and every academic and economic expression of our society—into every language, race, people and culture—and gathering this community.

One of the reasons that I hope to see you in church is that the old and young are there; professional people and laborers are there; people who are retired and people who are still studying are there; people with various ethnic backgrounds and community responsibilities are there. This gathering is the closest we can come in any neighborhood to the cross-section of the people of God who have this one thing in common: they recognize that God has loved them in Jesus Christ and they yield to the meaning of that recognition.

See you in church.

Not Welfare Recipients, but a Priesthood

So it is not groups, but a people that God is forming; and it is not welfare recipients, but a priesthood that God has chosen. Peter's doctrine of the church reminds us that it is to give, not to get, that we gather for worship in our local congregations.

The most common complaint I hear about church is, "I don't get anything out of it." When we judge church that way, we may be using, first of all, an *intellectual criterion.* Somehow that sermon is not as intellectually stimulating as it ought to be. And that may well be true.

Or we may be using an *emotional criterion,* "I don't feel any different afterwards; my feelings have been left unchanged." And it may be that they have.

Or, we may use an *esthetic criterion* to judge the church service, "I don't like the decor, the mood; I can't worship well in that setting. I don't like the music; it's too staid or too peppy." From the Gregorian Chant (which some people revel in and other people go to sleep by) to the hand-clapping of our pentecostal services, our esthetic expressions of worship are going to touch some people and leave others cold.

But the purpose of that gathering is not primarily intellectual, emotional or esthetic. Peter calls the church, in this passage, "a priesthood." He says "like living stones be yourselves built into a spiritual house, to be a *holy priesthood,* to offer spiritual *sacrifices* acceptable to God through Jesus Christ" (v. 5).

And as we gather Sunday by Sunday with this motley congregation, this reminder of the mixed multitude that God pulled out of Egypt in the Exodus, this raggedy band of forgiven sinners, we also gather as priests to offer sacrifices. And it's what we give that becomes important in our weekly worship.

See you in church.

This frantic seeking to have our needs met, this selfishness that masquerades as love, this attempt to bleed the experience for all that it is worth and somehow be nurtured by it, puts the emphasis in the wrong place. It is a futile quest for happiness. Happiness will only come as a by-product of worship and service.

Happiness is the other side of the coin of responsibility. The idea that we worship so that we can be turned on and jazzed up is asking of our worship something that it was never designed in the providence of God to do for us, except as a by-product of our devotion and adoration to God for what He Himself has done.

What happens, as we enter into this getting-and-not-giving mentality, as we become welfare recipients rather than a priesthood in our regular worship, is that we worship with a downcast eye. There is no way to look at my middle or anybody's without looking down. Navel contemplation, the compulsive concentration on your feelings or someone else's, is not a fitting substitute for worship. Back bent and eye downcast are not the postures of worship that the Bible itself describes to us.

Not groups but a people; not welfare recipients but a giving priesthood, a sacrificing priesthood—let's hear what the Bible is saying about the church.

See you in church.

Not a Sentimental Company, but a Divinely Ordered Reality

What is hardest for us to remember is that what the church of Christ is theologically, she really is.

In our frenzy, we often focus on trying to make the church something. And frequently we try to make the church be what we feel the church should be: a sentimental company, ruled by a tyranny of the emotions.

What the church is theologically is what she really is; the things unseen are eternal, and the true nature of the church is one of these eternal, unseen things, granted all her earthly expressions are flecked and marred, stained and tarred. There is no pure church this side of glory.

The church is the company of those who are built like living stones on a sure foundation.

It is the company of those who have made that terrifying choice to build on Jesus Christ rather than to cast Him aside as a rejected stone.

It is the company of those who have looked at Jesus Christ and declared precious Him whom some highly trained, deeply feeling, keenly skilled people have rejected.

It is the company of those who have in common only this faith and only this choice.

We look at the church and say, "The people are uptight, hypocritical, narrow, boring." And we select a little group from within the church about whom we feel very good and seek to sustain our spiritual lives in fellowship with them. As a means of fellowship and strength, groups are beautiful, one of the great things happening in our generation. But in no way do they take the place of the gathered congregation.

We have to move beyond the judgmental attitude that ranks Christians by whether they are open or not, whether we feel good about them or not. This is really a failure of forgiveness. It indicates that we have not fully received forgiveness because we have a hard time granting it. One of the heresies of the new fundamentalism is that we can accept almost everyone except Christians who are tied to the tradition.

As I said, this is where I came in, but there is no way for me to go out. God has chosen me to be part of His church. I am part of the church not of my choice but of His. I continue in the church, *not at my discretion but at His insistence.*

There is no other place to go. These are God's people and mine. This is what God is doing in history. This is the secret, the mystery, of the universe. This was the purpose for which everything was created: the people to serve and praise and glorify God.

The outcome of the church is already settled. The church will survive the new fundamentalism as it survived the old. It will be enriched by the new fundamentalism as it was enriched by the old. The outcome of the church is already settled; its perfection is assured; its ultimate destiny is fully determined.

The final chapters of the Bible picture it as it will be. And there you see an undifferentiated people—no groups, no categories, no cliques—an undifferentiated people before a throne, not gazing at their navels, not asking themselves how they feel about each other, but lifting their voices in adoration of almighty God and singing, "To him who sits upon the throne and to the Lamb be blessing and honor and glory and might for ever and ever!" (Rev. 5:13).

What the church is doing in heaven is what the

church should be doing on earth. Her ultimate style should be her interim mood.

It is God who is the center of the universe. It is God who is the focal point of our living. It is God who is the recipient of all worship and glory. And it is God upon whom our eyes should be fixed as we go to church week by week where we are.

See you in church.

I hope I've made myself clear. My deepest concern is not that your nonparticipation will destroy the church. My concern is for you, and it is more than a trivial one. I'm not merely echoing the notes of advice you have been given through the years by everyone from your early Sunday School teachers to the late J. Edgar Hoover. My point is not that going to church will enhance civic morality and reduce the crime rate, or that it will stabilize your marriage and promote your prosperity in your chosen vocation. It may well do all those. But if it didn't, you would have to go anyway.

Your regular participation in worship with your local congregation is the best indication that you have grasped the heart of the Christian message. Going to church does not make you a Christian. But Christian commitment is close to meaningless if you do not go. Worship with fellow worshipers comes nearer to describing what it means to be human than anything else you do. To shy away from this duty, to deprive yourselves of this privilege, is to fly the flag of human life at half-mast, no matter how bright its colors may appear.

See you in church.

Heavenly Father, I thank You for Your people, those I like and those I do not even know. To belong to Jesus and His church is life's greatest privilege. Help me really to believe this, and to express my belief by regular participation in worship with Your people, who have now become my people. Through Jesus Christ. Amen.

Ray C. Stedman

Topical Bible study to help students (high school to adult) discover and apply New Testament principles for the Body of Christ, the Church. Ray Stedman is pastor of Peninsula Bible Church, Palo Alto, Calif.

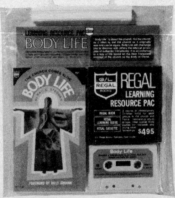

Pac includes Regal text, Learning Guide for individual response and resource cassette featuring interview with Ray Stedman and songs by John Fischer.

LEARNING RESOURCE PAC

G/L REGAL BOOKS ™

$4.95
(12 sessions)